dream it!
plan it!
do it!

dream it!
plan it!
do it!

Be your own
Life Coach

Diane M. Scholten

  A GODSFIELD BOOK

For my father, George R. Scholten, who was my first coach, remains my best coach and from whom I have learned not only how to succeed, but how to live a worthwhile life. And for my late mother, Jerrie G. Scholten, who taught me to love God, love family, and love to write.

First published in Great Britain in 2003
by Godsfield Press Ltd,
Laurel House, Station Approach,
Alresford, Hampshire SO24 9JH, U.K.

www.godsfieldpress.com

Project Editor: Sarah Doughty
Project Designers: Anna Hunter-Downing/Nicola Liddiard
Design Assistant: Ana Bjezancevic

Designed and produced for Godsfield Press
by The Bridgewater Book Company

2 4 6 8 10 9 7 5 3 1

Printed and bound in China

ISBN 1-84181-210-2

ACKNOWLEDGMENTS
So many people contributed their energy, ideas, and enthusiasm to make this book a reality. First, I'd like to acknowledge my longtime friend and accountant, Marilyn Hollinger, who suggested the original workbook, from which this book was derived. She said "you've got a lot of good materials, why don't you pull it together and publish it?" So I did and learned a lot in the process.

I received significant help on the first version from friends and colleagues who reviewed the manuscript and gave me suggestions. Thanks especially to Ann Hughes, Mary Lou Johns, Susan Spritz-Myers, Susan Johnson, and my dear friend and former partner, Sue McGill.

I thank all of my clients, with whom I've fine-tuned these tools, with a special tip of the hat to those on whose stories the case studies in this book are based. This includes Lois Haubold, Bill Haubold, Terry Keleher, Lisa Padden, and Phil Arnold, and also those who have chosen to remain anonymous. Also thanks to my niece Courtney Keegan and my cousin JoAnne Glasgow on whom I very loosely modeled their namesakes in the book. Thanks as well to Aaron Rosen and Pat Michelsen for their generous input. Thanks to Sharon Dorr, Sarah Doughty, Mark Truman, Lucia Watson, and all the great folks at Godsfield, Bridgewater, and Penguin who have worked hard to make this book a reality.

Without the help, encouragement and love of my family and friends this book would not exist. My late mother loved to write and influenced me as a woman and a writer. My beloved dad continues to encourage me and give me great advice. My siblings Jean Harhai, George Scholten, and Pier Keegan have been marvelous. And my beloved friends Bill Wallenbecker, Pat Michelsen, Barbara Poole, Susan Spritz-Myers, Julia Mossbrige, Paula Hardin, Eric Dean and so many other wonderful ones (forgive me for not mentioning all of you!) have cheered me on, given me feedback and overall brought me joy. As has my dear little cat, Caitlin Marie.

Lastly, and very importantly, to wonderful Brenda Rosen, editor extraordinaire, fellow Mystery School attendee, and the one who truly made all of this possible. This absolutely would not exist in this form without you, Brenda—thank you!

Contents

Introduction

*I*f you're ready to rebuild your life from the foundations up, this book is for you. If it feels as though the life you're living needs a major remodeling, keep reading. This book grew directly out of my coaching practice. I use these very same techniques with my coaching clients and in my workshops. But before I tried these tools and techniques on others, I used them on myself. Quite simply, they work.

You can be your own coach. You can redesign your life, starting with **EXACTLY** what life presents to you today. You can begin by reading this book, doing the exercises, and being willing to dream a bigger dream for yourself—that is, a vision of how you'd wish your life to be. Then, by making plans to achieve that dream and getting into incremental action—you really can change your life.

This book will show you how. It will guide you, not only with ideas, but with examples of how it has worked for others. And it will provide step-by-step instructions that you can use in **YOUR** life.

Dream It! Plan It! Do It! You can enjoy both the creativity and the big-picture thinking that are a part of creating a wider vision for yourself as well as the structured analytical thinking you use in planning. But the key element in making your dreams come true lies in neither dreaming nor planning, though both are absolutely necessary. Without a big dream, you don't have anything concrete to strive toward. It's similar to your vision of a beautiful new home you'd like to live in. The plans you make are like the blueprints to build the house. But **YOU STILL HAVE TO MOVE FORWARD TO GET THERE.** The vision and the blueprints won't mean a thing unless you get into action. As one of my clients used to say, "Action leads to satisfaction."

So, are you ready to move into the life of your dreams? Even if you don't know what that life would look like, are you willing to find out? Are you willing to believe, as so many have done before you, that if you dream it and plan it, you can **DO** it?

Well, then—let's go!

How to Use This Book

*T*his book will give you the tools you need to envision the life you want to live, map out a plan to get there, and get support as you move toward your ideal lifestyle.

You may use this book in a linear fashion, just as it is laid out: start with Chapter 1, read the text, complete the exercises, and move on. If you've picked up the book because you're ready to create a new life for yourself, this may be the best bet for you.

I recommend that all readers begin with Part One. Even if you feel certain that you know where you're at right now, there is great value in getting it down on paper. The tools in Getting Started—Who Am I Right Now? will clarify your current situation and give you a strong foundation for moving forward into creating your new life.

Maybe you are great at envisioning future possibilities. You already know how you want your life to be, even though, at the present moment, it is less than satisfactory. Perhaps you've known for years. You, dear reader, are already an expert at imagining a better life. For you, completing Part One to clarify where you are now and then moving on to Part Three: Plan It! How Do I Get There? may be the best bet.

I've worked with clients who are fabulous project managers. Some of them do this job for a living and can map out a plan for any endeavor; it comes naturally for them. Some of these brilliant planners and implementers are also great at visioning and getting the big picture. Some, however, are not. If that's you, then once you figure out where you're starting from, Part Two will help you to envision your ideal life. While you may want to do the activities and exercises in Part Three (they'll be easy and fun if you fit this profile), you may have a way of project planning that has worked for years. If so, use it, make your plan your way, and then move on to Part Four for some great get-into-action tips.

Some of us learn from examples—real-world stories of people who have done what we'd like to do. If you'd like to see the examples first and then have the theory and exercises, start with Part Five: Life Coach Studies. You'll see examples of how others have used these very same tools and techniques to change their lives. Then, based on what you learn, you can go back to the earlier parts of the book and do the work you need to do to move into the life you want to create.

A last word about how to use this book: While its intent is to give you all the tools and techniques you need to be your own life coach, that doesn't preclude using it with another coach, if you have one. Or you might want to do the activities with a friend, or even a group of friends.

When I teach my class, "How to Become a Professional Life Coach," I encourage the participants to get a coaching buddy and practice some of the skills they've learned. Similarly, in my workshop, "Creating Your Ideal Life," we do exercises in a group setting and have the added benefit of discussing our findings together. The synergy and support that a group provides can really propel you forward. And working with others—a coach, a friend, a group of friends—provides the accountability that has helped so many coaching clients move ahead.

However you use this book, I encourage you to get the most out of it by **ACTUALLY DOING THE EXERCISES**! Reading it will give you ideas and the hope that you truly can create the life you desire, but the way to get there is through action. Let's start by taking an inventory of where you're at right now. What's the foundation you'll be building on? We'll find out in Part One.

So, if you're ready to stop wishing (or, worse, kvetching and complaining!), and start doing, then it's time to begin our adventure.

Getting Started

WHO AM I RIGHT NOW?

*I*f building the life you'd love to inhabit is like building a new home, this part is the preconstruction phase. Who are you right now? What are your foundations? The assessment tools and journaling exercises here will give you the starting point from which you will begin the journey to creating a New You.

Why is this step so important? It's because without a realistic assessment of your current life—what's working as well as what's not—you don't know where you're starting from. Additionally, analyzing your current situation and who you are right now will help you figure out what you really want in life.

Some people feel an ideal life—one that is totally unrelated to where they are now—is out there just waiting for them.

This is foolish.

Your ideal life may well be very different from the life you are living now in many ways. But the seeds of your future are right here now. How are you going to get to be the New You with the new life? Simple—start from where you are. Right here. Right now.

There's real power in writing things down. You may **THINK** you know what your life is like right now, how you spend your time, and what's important to you.

But if you're like most of my clients—and like me—actually doing these exercises and writing down your findings will yield some insights and possibly some surprises.

You may discover that your current life is better than you thought it was. Or you may find you've been fooling yourself in saying, "Aw, it's not **THAT** bad."

Maybe you're disgusted and feel like nothing is working, and you think "I just want to start all over." You may be surprised to see that some tiny corners of your life RIGHT NOW contain the way you want to live in the future.

In Chapter 1, we're going to do some detailed digging. The assessment tools will help you get a clear picture of where you are in many key areas. We're going to take the blinders off and look at your life, straight on. We'll see what's there, what's working for you, and what's not.

The next step in laying out your foundations is to clean up the mess! In Chapter 2 (based on what you learned in Chapter 1), you're going to further your inventory by figuring out what you need to clean up, clear out, and eliminate. Creativity comes out of the void. We need to welcome your new life by making room for it. I once had a friend who, when she wanted a new partner in her life, would begin by clearing out space in her closets and home. It signified that she was also clearing out a space in her heart. She created emptiness so that she could fill her life with what she really wanted.

Part One gives you a current snapshot of your life. It's like a prelude to Part Two: Dream It!—Where Do I Want to Go?

Chapter 2 gives you the first part of your plan—clearing away the clutter and being ruthless in making space and time for your new life. In that way, it's a prelude to both Part Three: Plan It!—How Do I Get There? and Part Four: Do It!—How Do I Get into Action?

So Part One really sets the tone for your work as your own life coach. Please, do yourself a favor and don't skip the exercises in this section. No, it doesn't count if you just read it and think about it. Write things down! Get into action!

CHAPTER 1

Before you begin construction, it's important to know what you have to work with. Upon what foundation will your new life be built? You'll begin with assessing all the elements of your life right now. Some you will want to keep. Other aspects (people, situations, things) are ripe for elimination. And some parts of your life you'll want to keep but alter in some way, large or small. But first you must know where you stand.

A WALK around *the Property*

WHAT DO I HAVE TO BUILD ON?

𝒯he self-assessment tools in this chapter will give you a clear picture of where you're at right now. You'll assess your foundations in eight key areas:

1. Career
2. Money
3. Health & Fitness
4. Friends & Family

5. Physical Environment
6. Romance
7. Fun & Recreation
8. Personal Growth & Spiritual Development

I have found in years of coaching clients that just having the courage (and taking the time) to look at what's actually going on can be a huge catalyst for change. If you've been avoiding introspection, this chapter may uncover the reason for it. And knowledge is power. Once you know where you're at right now, you can more clearly see what you'd like to change.

Assessing your Foundations
THE WHEEL OF LIFE

When Lisa came to me as a client, she felt both enthusiastic and overwhelmed. In her twenties and in a new, promising career, she felt her life both full of possibilities and full of confusion. She knew there was more she wanted—to meet the man of her dreams, to have a more meaningful career, to own a new car and eventually a house—but she had no idea where to begin.

*L*isa first needed a high level overview of her life right now. For that, I use a tool called the "Wheel of Life," which I first learned about in my training from the Coaches Training Institute. The wheel of life is divided into eight foundation areas. These are the key areas of your life which you will assess.

Here's how it works: For each area of life, assess where you are RIGHT NOW on a scale of 0–10, where 0 is the worst things could be and 10 is the best. Using 0 as the center of the wheel (where the spokes come together) and 10 as the outer perimeter, place a dot in the appropriate place for that section, with the numeric rating next to it. For example, let's say Lisa rates herself as follows:

Career—5, Money—4, Health & Fitness—9,
Friends & Family—9, Physical Environment—6,
Romance—2, Fun & Recreation—8,
Personal Growth & Spiritual Development—9

When Lisa completed ranking each area, she connected the dots, creating a visual representation of the balance in her life.

A Picture of the Balance in Your Own Wheel of Life

$\mathcal{N}$ow, use the wheel to assess where **YOU** are in each area, following the instructions on the previous page. First, rate each area individually (remember, 0 or 1 is low and 10 is high). Write the numeric rating next to the dot. When you've filled in all eight areas, connect the dots.

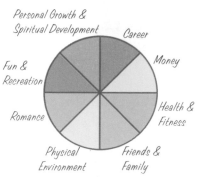

Personal Growth & Spiritual Development — *Career* — *Money* — *Health & Fitness* — *Friends & Family* — *Physical Environment* — *Romance* — *Fun & Recreation*

Here's how to approach this. Let's say that right now you make enough money to get by—you can pay your monthly bills and have a little left over for fun. But you can't really save for bigger things or do anything big. So maybe you'd rate money a "5"—it's okay, but not great. Or, say, you just bought the home of your dreams and you're having a ball decorating it—maybe your physical environment feels like a "10" right now—it's perfect! Or, maybe you've been single **WAY** too long and wish you had a partner—for you, romance might feel like a big fat "0." Bear in mind this is how **YOU** feel subjectively. I've done this exercise with clients and laughed when one woman said "Romance. Hmm, I just got divorced and that feels like a 10 to me—free at last!"

So how does your wheel look? If it is not smooth, it shows your life is out of balance—a bumpy ride! After this initial assessment you will focus on each area, and build foundations.

Before You Build a Castle, Check out the Foundations

$\mathcal{Y}$ou wouldn't dream of beginning to build a castle without first laying a good solid foundation, would you? Similarly, before you move into the castle of your ideal life, it's good to know your starting point. Over the next 16 pages you'll see how some of my clients assessed their foundations in the various areas of life, and then you'll take inventory of your own current state. In each case, please describe in detail what your foundation is. Give a specific picture of where you're starting from. Taking the time to accurately and frankly look at where you are is the first step toward building the life of your dreams.

Be thorough. Be brave. It's time to get real!

Foundations *Career*

When you think about work do you sing "Here Comes the Sun" or "Take this Job and Shove It"? Work is a huge part of our lives and a key element in our satisfaction. If you're newly out of college, just getting a job and learning about the work world may be enough to keep you interested. For many people, learning is a key part of career satisfaction—and sometimes that wanes as our careers advance.

As you assess your career, look for these intangibles as well as the types of things you'd put on a resumé—educational background, specific skills, etc. There are key questions to ask that help you to focus on your foundations for work.

For each foundation, I will show you how one of my clients has answered the questions on the facing page. Then it's your turn!

Ken's Case Study

Here's an example of how my client Ken, a midlife career changer, assessed his career:

- *I have a good background in engineering: a master's degree. My early career in electrical engineering design and positions in aerospace was successful.*

- *I have always been interested in the technical side of things. As a kid I wanted to design spaceships!*

- *I have good connections with professional groups in the field of engineering based on many years of experience.*

- *I've had a series of senior engineering management roles at a large corporation, but I miss the technical side of things, which I am good at.*

- *I AM enthusiastic about the possibility of more technical content in my future work. This could translate into career options. But I don't want a new career to be seen as "stepping down" from a managerial position, and I am concerned about the financial implications.*

YOUR TURN!

🦋 *What education do you have that serves as a career foundation? Think out of the box—not just university, but technical training, on the job training, etc.*

_____

_____

_____

🦋 *What do you LOVE to do? What would you do even if you didn't get paid? When you were a kid, what did you say you wanted to be when you grew up?*

_____

_____

_____

🦋 *Who do you hang out with? That is, what networks, associations, or groups are you part of that enhance your current (or future) career?*

_____

_____

🦋 *What are you good at? Yes, pull out your resumé to get some clues—let's start there:*

_____

_____

🦋 *But also, what else are you good at that could translate into career options?*

_____

_____

🦋 *Given all these wondrous skills, talents, and abilities, please write out on a separate piece of paper 20 different career paths or jobs you could pursue using these talents. Be a fashion designer, a newspaper columnist, a film director! Include some jobs that you'd never do, but that you would qualify for. Be wild! Be bold! If you really want to shine, go for 50 different career paths!*

Self-Assessment: What did I learn?

Okay, now you've had a chance to reflect on your career foundations. Take a moment to reread what you've written and to reflect. What surprises you? What feels good to you? What feels tired and worn-out? If a career coach were to read what you wrote as your career foundation, what do you think he or she would tell you? Choose three career options from your list of 20 (or 50!) and take out relevant books on those careers from your local library.

Foundations

Money

oney! We love it, we hate it, we wish we had more of it. In a culture that equates money with value, it is a loaded symbol indeed. As you assess this part of your life, remember to simply assess your current total financial foundations without judgment. What are your assets? What do you owe? If you have $6,000 in your savings account but forget your $43,000 credit card debt you're getting a skewed picture. Be brave! Facing the facts will help you achieve your financial goals.

Dawn's Case Study

Let's look at how my client, Dawn, a recently divorced single mom in her early thirties answered questions on the facing page:

🐷 Right now, I make about $2,000/month from my freelance graphic design work. My monthly child-support check is $1,200.

🐷 I have a small amount in a savings account.

🐷 No other savings or investments, unfortunately!

🐷 I get half of Roger's pension, now in a self-directed IRA.

🐷 My parents regularly give me and my son Daniel cash gifts—this helps pay for his education.

🐷 I have a 2001 Honda Civic and it's in good working order—this is an asset, which I want to keep. However, I have a lot of stuff that I don't need that is valuable. (I could try and sell stuff I don't need on eBay; that should raise some cash to help short term.).

🐷 My monthly mortgage payment is $1,150 (I need to get this down!), plus living expenses on top.

🐷 My credit card debt is $6,900.

🐷 I do need to find reliable funding to secure Daniel's educational future, without relying on my parents.

YOUR TURN!

🛍 Okay, let's start with the basics. How much money do you make right now?

🛍 How much do you have in your checking account and in your savings account?

🛍 Do you have other savings or investments?

🛍 I know, I know, you're FAR too young to even be thinking about retirement, but IS there any money set aside for your elder years or will you work until you drop?

🛍 And if you have kids, how is their college education funded?

🛍 How about your stuff? What material assets do you have? Cars? Planes? Boats? Big diamonds? Hmm… well, list the stuff that's worthwhile here:

🛍 Now onto the less cheery side of tracking your money: What you owe. How much do you pay in rent? Got a mortgage or loans? How much is it? What are your living expenses?

🛍 Credit card debt? Go ahead, take a look. Be brave, write down here how much you owe to whom:

🛍 What else do you want to put down about your financial foundations?

Self-Assessment: What did I learn?

In the absence of a financial guru, your accountant or Santa Claus looking over shoulder, what can YOU deduce from what you just wrote? How are you doing financially? Will the foundation you have established take you where you want to go? If not, do you know what you need to change to get there? What made you most proud as you reread this section? What makes you most worried? Take a moment to reflect on what you learned from this exercise. Consider how to improve your situation— either with the professional help of your financial planner if you need further advice, or through personal action such as selling unwanted valuable goods on the Internet or in your local paper.

Foundations

Health & FITNESS

It really is true. Health is probably your most important asset. Regardless of your age or occupation, without health and sufficient energy everything is much harder. You may never stop to appreciate the foundations you have in this area. But smart people pay attention to their health, knowing it is key to a full, thriving life.

Ann's Case Study

Ann, whom you'll meet again in the Case Studies (page 142), is in her forties, very successful and hard working. She knows that good health is a key element to her success. In response to the questions on the following page, she wrote:

🐾 I try and keep myself in top physical condition.

🐾 I get at least 8 hours of sleep per night. I really need this rest to thrive.

🐾 I eat healthfully, even when traveling or entertaining.

🐾 I DO work out, even if it's just a brisk walk, at least 2 or 3 times each week. This keeps me trim.

🐾 I get regular checkups.

🐾 I do things for my emotional health, too: journaling frequently, and spending time with family and friends.

🐾 I have been putting off dealing with my frequent migraines—I'm not sure what to do about these.

🐾 Finally, massage, tennis, and golf are GREAT for my physical and mental well-being, and I plan to do more. Also I want to meditate.

YOUR TURN!

🏸 *What's the current state of your health?*

_____

🏸 *How well do you sleep?*

_____

🏸 *What about your eating habits?*

_____

🏸 *Are you the correct weight and in shape?*

_____

🏸 *Are you getting regular health checkups?*

_____

🏸 *How's your emotional well-being? Think about your stress levels, your moods, and your energy levels. Are you active and energetic or are you always tired?*

_____

_____

🏸 *What have you been putting off dealing with? Come on, I know there's something you've been meaning to do to improve your physical condition. What is it?*

_____

_____

_____

What else can you do to improve your most important asset, your health?

_____

_____

_____

Self-Assessment: What did I learn?

Okay, take a moment to read over what you wrote. How are you feeling? Does what you just read about your health reflect someone who really loves and cares for themself? Would your mother be proud of you if she read this? More importantly, are YOU proud of how you care for your physical being? What did doing this exercise teach you? Book an appointment with your doctor to assess your state of health and ask for advice in improving it. Consider your diet and plan a week of healthy dishes to get you into the pattern of healthy eating.

Foundations

Friends & FAMILY

You tell your husband you love him. You quickly kiss the kids good night. You send your mother flowers on her birthday and take Dad out to lunch. You call your friends regularly and have them round for dinner. But have you ever stopped to look at who is in your life and how these people—your family and friends—enhance your existence?

Take time to list the people who nourish you, starting with your family, then your closest friends, and on out to the more outer circle of friends/acquaintances. Are there people in your family or circle of friends who are a negative influence? Note that here, also.

Joe's Case Study

My client Joe, a young, hard-working software engineer in London, felt very blessed with his young and growing family. However, his busy lifestyle made him feel cut off from his friends. Here's how he tallied up this key part of his life in response to the questions on the following page:

🐾 *My wife, Alicia. (Marrying her was the single smartest thing I've ever done!). Our daughter, Elise and our new baby son, Ian.*

🐾 *I'm close to my mother and my brother, Mark. Alicia's parents live in Manchester, so we don't see them as much, but we can often see my mother and Mark.*

🐾 *Our families are at the center of our life. Our closest friends live near by and also have kids.*

🐾 *Probably the guys from my soccer club. I used to love to go out for a beer after our games.*

🐾 *My colleagues from work.*

🐾 *There's one relationship that I'm concerned about. Alicia's brother Nigel is running with a fast crowd, and is NOT a role model I'd want for the kids at the moment. However, I don't want to cut him out of our lives completely.*

YOUR TURN!

🔖 *Who do you love the most? Write the names of the people in your family who you are closest to and say what they mean to you.*

_____

_____

_____

🔖 *Who else are you close to?*

_____

_____

_____

🔖 *If you had a big circle and your family and closest friends were at the center (call this your "A" list), who would be in the innermost layer? Why?*

_____

_____

🔖 *Who'd be in the next rung out? (Call this your "B" list!)*

_____

_____

🔖 *Who fits into the acquaintances category?*

_____

_____

🔖 *Does anybody need to be removed? Are you holding on to dead friendships just because they are familiar? Explain if there are relationships that you would rather let go of and why.*

_____

_____

Self-Assessment: What did I learn?

Whom DO you love? Who loves you? What did this exercise teach you? Are there enough names in your circle of life? What feelings came up as you did this? Gratitude? Nostalgia? Delight? Regret? Think about what you learned from this. Consider how you can spend more time with those closest to you and how to reduce the time you spend with people who are a negative influence—or how you would let go of them completely.

Foundations

Physical

ENVIRONMENT

*A*s you assess your physical environment foundations, take a good look at your living quarters (house, apartment, houseboat—wherever you live!). What's working in your environment? What's not? Is your space big enough? Tidy enough? In a good location? Needing repairs? Decorated to delight you? What about your "stuff"? Look at your entire physical environment—how is it serving you and how is it not?

Ted's Case Study

Ted is a single gay man in his thirties. He has a busy career, is dating, and has a big family nearby. Ted also has a home environment that is not totally working for him, as you'll see from his answers to the questions on the following page:

🐾 *I like my house—it's a bit old and needs repairs, but it's basically structurally sound and I love its architectural details.*

🐾 *I really love my neighborhood. The houses are all unique and I love living in such a hip, gay-friendly, and upscale town.*

🐾 *Now, on to the challenges! I have too much stuff. My home office is a disaster! The basement is filled with "someday-I-may-need-this" stuff. I have too many clothes and old papers.*

🐾 *I have really gotten the maximum usage out of my car. It's way past time to buy a new one—this has to be top priority. I'd also like to redo the kitchen—now is the time to move into action. And, I'd like a new couch, although I don't really need one. Finally, I really need a new leather jacket or get the old one repaired.*

YOUR TURN!

📖 *What do you like about YOUR current physical environment (your home)?*

_____

_____

_____

_____

📖 *What do you like (or dislike) about your neighborhood?*

_____

_____

_____

_____

📖 *What do you need to physically change about your home? Think about your office, your closet, your storage areas. What's under your bed that needs clearing out?*

_____

_____

_____

_____

📖 *Think about the other things you need to make your home environment better. Think about how you would prioritize this list; what you would action first, and why.*

_____

_____

_____

_____

Self-Assessment: What did I learn?

So you've just done a little archaeological dig through your living environment. What did you find? Is there an orderly civilization living in this home or is it the land of complete chaos? After rereading what you just wrote, what's the dominant feeling you get? What do you most want to rush out and do right now? If you are unhappy with your home and neighborhood, consider the possibility of moving house. If you are basically happy with these factors, make a list of ten actions that would improve your physical environment—and do the first two today!

Foundations

Romance

Ah, love! Maybe you're searching for a partner. Perhaps you've been married for weeks, months or even for decades. Maybe you're going through a relationship breakup and are not sure about the future. Some of you may be single and want to stay that way, but for many of us this is a key area of life that has tremendous bearing on our happiness.

Courtney's Case Study

Courtney is twenty-two, a new university graduate and just embarking on her career in marketing. She wants a serious relationship. Here's how she responded to the questions on the following page:

🏵 I have had relationships in the past that were not too serious. I now know that I DO want to meet "Mr. Right."

🏵 I've made a list of what I'm looking for in a guy—from physical characteristics (he has to be tall!), to things about his interests (loves basketball and reading) and his character (honest, loyal, family-centered).

🏵 I also know what my assets are: I'm pretty, smart, hard working, and lots of fun!

🏵 One thing couples can work on is to communicate well. Good communication makes any relationship stronger.

🏵. I have a dating plan. I also count my wide circle of friends as a foundation: They are sources for blind dates, but also, since I have emotional connections with my gang, I am not so emotionally needy.

YOUR TURN!

🐾 *On a separate sheet of paper make a list of all the people you've had romantic relationships with.*

🐾 *Circle the relationships that were important, meaningful—more than just casual dating.*

🐾 *Next to each circled name write down the top three things you learned by being in a relationship with this person.*

🐾 *What patterns did you see in your relationships, if any?*

_____

_____

🐾 *Now, write a list of attributes you're looking for in a potential partner (or in your current partner if you're in a relationship). Shoot for the moon and stars!*

_____

_____

🐾 *And a list of what you think you have to contribute to a relationship—be thorough.*

_____

_____

🐾 *Whether or not you have a partner, what is the single most important thing you think YOU can do to make any relationship stronger?*

_____

🐾 *If you don't have a partner and want one, what is your plan to meet Mr. or Ms. Right?*

_____

_____

Self-Assessment: What did I learn?

Ooh, boy! That was digging deep, yes? This is a sensitive area for most of us, one that we hold rather close to our hearts. What happened when you reread this? What did doing this exercise teach you? What emotions came up? What have you learned? Consider how you would meet someone with the attributes you are looking for. For example, if you're looking for a sporty person, is there a local sports club with social events you could join with a friend?

Foundations

Fun

& RECREATION

*M*y younger clients could mentor my midlife clients on fun and recreation. As life's responsibilities increase, fun is often the thing that gets knocked off our radar screens. Do you know what is fun for you? Do you have fun? Look over your calendar or your journal—what have you been up to lately that could qualify as fun (no, checking your email out on the deck instead of in your office doesn't count!). Do you have hobbies that you used to enjoy which could be resurrected? Take a good look at what you're doing now to relax and renew—and what you'd like to be doing.

Mike's Case Study

Mike found that his life was full all right—but not of recreation. He is a busy sales guy with a wife and two daughters. When Mike and I looked at his life, we saw a big gaping hole in the arena of fun. Here was his starting point:

🛩 Well, I still have all my RC (remote control) airplane stuff!

🛩 I enjoyed sports in high school, and having fun with friends.

🛩 I've made a list of activities I enjoy, including the gym, basketball, and reading but I know I NEED to devote energy to fun and "Mike time." ·

🛩 I have a group of friends with similar interests. My fun tends to be fairly physical, so playing basketball with the guys is a possibility. I'd also love to go fly fishing.

🛩 I'd like to set up some regular 'blading dates with my daughter Danielle—she loves rollerblading as much as I do and it makes her laugh as well.

🛩 I love to be the life and soul of the party. My friends can tell you some stories!

YOUR TURN!

🔖 *What did you do for fun when you were a kid?*

_____

_____

_____

🔖 *How about high school, college, and in your 20s?*

_____

_____

_____

🔖 *What do you do for fun now? List 12 things that you've done for fun or leisure in the last three months.*

_____

_____

_____

_____

_____

🔖 *Do you have any creative hobbies or other activities you regularly pursue?*

_____

_____

🔖 *What else can you do to improve your fun and recreation time? You don't need to be serious—you can include things that would make your friends or family laugh!*

_____

🔖 *Are you the life of the party or the designated party pooper? How would we know that? Why? Are you happy in this role?*

_____

Self-Assessment: What did I learn?

Girls (and boys) just want to have fun! So, do you? What did this exercise teach you about yourself? What inspirations did you get from doing this? What are you likely to do differently as a result of assessing these foundations? If you need physical fun with friends, make a sporting date. If you need more "you" time, set aside an evening for a visit to the movies, a stroll in the park, woods, or along the beach.

Foundations
Personal Growth
& SPIRITUAL DEVELOPMENT

Personal growth and spiritual development mean different things to different people. For some, spirituality is simply practicing the religion of their youth. For different people, or at different points in life, the spiritual quest is a side-dish. For other people, or at other times, it is both the main dish and the dessert. What helps you to be your best self? How do you want to grow and evolve? What guides your philosophy, values, and morals?

Joanne's Case Study

At fifty-seven and recently widowed, Joanne, a university professor, found herself in a huge transition period. This led her into a period of intense questing for meaning in her life. Here was her starting point:

🔖 *I said goodbye to spirituality when I left the Anglican religion of my youth. Now it's time to change all this.*

🔖 *I recently started teaching comparative religion after years of English teaching, and this has made me think more deeply. It's as if my soul knew what was coming.*

🔖 *I am seeking personal and spiritual growth through workshops and reading groups.*

🔖 *I have a meditation practice.*

🔖 *I used to do yoga and found it meditative. There is a yoga center near the university, where I could practice.*

🔖 *My cousin attended a spiritual retreat and is sending me the audiotapes. I may ask my friend Marie, if she would be a spiritual mentor to me.*

YOUR TURN!

* Did you grow up in a particular religion or spiritual tradition? Which one?

_____

_____

* How are your spiritual needs different today?

_____

_____

_____

* What are you seeking in your spiritual life?

_____

_____

_____

* What activities do you regularly practice to help you grow and deepen?

_____

_____

_____

* Do you pray? Meditate? Do yoga, t'ai chi or other meditative movements?

_____

_____

_____

* What classes, groups, authors, musicians—what outside sources, overall—could you learn the most from?

_____

_____

_____

Self-Assessment: What did I learn?

Are you a lifelong learner? Are you a spiritual seeker? Does this part of your life—your soul's growth, and your own pathway to greatness—get the attention it needs? As you reread what you wrote, what comes up for you? Consider visiting a place of worship—church, synagogue, mosque—or a spiritually uplifting outdoor space to contemplate the meaning of spirituality in your life.

Taking Inventory

WHAT HAVE I LEARNED?

Just as prudent builders periodically take inventory in the course of a building project, you too should stop along the way to summarize and deepen your understanding. Take some time now to stop and reflect on what you've read and the exercises you've done in this chapter. The purpose of the Inventory at the end of this chapter and at the end of the first four parts of the book, is to deepen your learning through reflection.

Ask yourself:

• Were you surprised by what you found when you took the time to look at these different areas of your life? What surprised you?
• In which areas are your foundations strongest? Why is this so?
• Which areas need the most attention? Are these the same areas that ALWAYS get less focus in your life?
• What's your reaction to what you've learned? Are you excited? Encouraged? Discouraged? Overwhelmed? How did doing this make you FEEL? If you are fired up and raring to go, that's great!

If you're feeling a little discouraged or overwhelmed, don't despair! In the next chapter you will learn how to prioritize and make a start on clearing out the clutter as your first step to a better life.

_____

_____

_____

_____

_____

_____

_____

_____

_____

_____

_____

_____

_____

_____

_____

_____

_____

_____

> You're beginning to get excited about the New You you're about to build. You have a feel for the ground upon which you stand. But look around. There's litter on your beautiful lot! This chapter will focus on clearing out old issues, tasks, and anything that is in the way, prior to beginning. The tools in this chapter help you list what needs to be cleared out and get started on cleaning up the mess.

CLEARING the brush
Cleaning up
BEFORE BUILDING SOMETHING NEW

*Y*ou know what they are—the nagging items you keep putting off. The things you'll get to "someday." The physical clutter, administrative disorganization, unreturned phone calls or emails, the maintenance chores (change the oil in the car, update your will) that never seem to get done. Maybe it's things that are broken and need to be fixed. Maybe it's a half-done creative project that you really want to finish, but . . .

Remember Ted from "Foundations: Physical Environment" (page 24)? He made a list of what needed to be cleared up, cleaned out, or eliminated, not only in his physical environment, but in ALL elements of his life. In the next few pages, we'll look at Ted's list and then you'll start your own. Remember, right now we're just making a list. Action will follow, but first let's get it down on paper.

Clearing the brush
MAKING A LIST

First, Ted started with his home. He went through each room in his house and made a list of things he wanted to get rid of, organize, fix, etc. This included his closets and drawers. The storage areas were particularly filled with opportunities to purge!

Other clutter that needed purging was information: papers, his address book, and his computer files. None of these had been purged in living memory. One step Ted took was to unsubscribe from all computer lists in which he no longer wanted to participate.

Then Ted tackled a deeper level: people. I encouraged him to make a list of the people in his life now and consider it seriously. With whom was he was spending time, and how was that for him? Ted has a sister, Tracy, who is emotionally draining. He is committed to maintaining closeness with his family, and he certainly didn't want to eliminate Tracy from his life. But he DID want to change the frequency of his connections with her and enhance the quality of them.

When Ted thought about his friends and coworkers, he realized there were a few people

*T*ake a look at Ted's Case Study (sidebar). At first Ted was reluctant to take off the blinders and **REALLY** look at what needed to be tackled in his life. He knew that his physical clutter was interfering with his productivity and serenity. He balked at the idea that he needed to do a LOT of clearing out of the old before he could welcome the new. However, after he cleaned his home office and experienced a surge of energy, enthusiasm, and optimism, Ted was a believer.

Ted felt a bit overwhelmed both before and after he wrote out his list (see pages 38–39). But with my guidance, he systematically got all of it down on paper. And then he had a great starting point from which to clear things up.

Are you ready to get started? Here's how to begin. Get a pad of paper and a pen. Like Ted, we'll start at the very basic physical he didn't want to spend time with anymore. Having lunch with his colleague Mitch, for instance, had become a habit, but not one with any life left in it. He decided to let this relationship die off naturally.

His old college friend Jake had continually used Ted over the years. He called Ted only when he needed something, did a lot of complaining, and was never there when Ted wanted to talk or needed a favor. Ted decided to be tough and tell Jake he really didn't want to continue the friendship. That felt both scary and enormously liberating.

The next level of things to eliminate were some bad habits. Ted knew that his gotta-have-it-every night bowl of ice cream wasn't serving him well: Now that he was in his thirties, the ice cream was beginning to show up around his waistline. He didn't want to give up totally on his favorite treat, so he decided to cut back.

At a spiritual level, Ted took a look at his self-limiting and self-defeating beliefs. The breakup of his last relationship had left him feeling unlovable. He decided to work on letting go of the belief that he was unworthy of love. He also realized that he was too judgmental and decided to put that on his elimination list, too.

level—your home. Room by room, systematically make a list of what needs to be organized, fixed, replaced, or eliminated. Include your closets, drawers, secret cubby-holes. You may find some huge "purging" opportunities in your storage areas.

You may find that you'd rather **DO IT** than list it—if you're ready to tackle one room or your home you can separate the items in the room into four piles: Keep As Is, Keep and Fix, Throw Out, and Donate/Sell. Notice there is **NOT** a pile that says "Figure Out Later"! Be bold and be brave! Feng shui teaches us that a lot of clutter laying around saps our energy. Purge and feel a surge of creativity, energy, and life. Some people believe that making space in your home opens you up for new opportunities. Get ready!

Once you've cleared your physical clutter, you can move on to something slightly less concrete: your information overload clutter. You know what I'm talking about: your computer files, your digital address book, your numbers stored in your cell phone, your address book. Maybe you're signed up on a bunch of listserves or get 'e-zines you never read. All those emails that you automatically delete not only clutter up your electronic wastebasket, but, if you're like most of us, you have that moment of regret "hmm, I ought to read this" or "I need to get around to unsubscribing…" Well, today's the day! And, on the border between information and physical stuff are magazines, newspapers, etc. What are you going to read "Someday"? What articles have you clipped "for when I need them, later" or "when I have the time to read them"? Come on! Clear room for new ideas! Get rid of information clutter and see your mind become clearer, too!

Ready to go deeper? How about looking at not only **WHAT** is in your life but also **WHO**. Are there people in your life who are there only because they always have been? That former colleague or your neighbor from three moves ago? If these relationships still nurture you or serve a meaningful purpose in your life, by all means keep them! But many times we have people in our lives who get in the way of our growth but we're too wimpy to end the relationships. This is the hardest level of "clearing the clutter" (and I know—that sounds cold-hearted!) but it is the one that produces the most dramatic results. Ask yourself: When the phone rings who do I hope it will NOT be? Which people do I have in my life but would cross the street to avoid? With whom is "duty" or "obligation" the driver for getting together?

Changing the people in your life is a more challenging growth opportunity than cleaning your closets. After all, we're talking about other people here. Be kind. Be gentle. But be decisive. If the relationship is dead, gently let it go.

Ted's initial list

Clean out my office!

Get boxes off floor in dining room.

Go through piles of paper and files in filing cabinet.

Tackle the computer files, too!

Clean the basement.

Clean my address book.

Get off all those e-lists I no longer read.

Get my car serviced.

Buy new jeans and a cotton sweater.

Figure out what to do about Tracy.

Graciously get out of weekly lunches with Mitch.

Say goodbye to Jake!

Get my toe back into dating— maybe sign up with an online service, try "speed-dating"?

Complete writing project at work.

Write more chapters for the book I'm coauthoring with colleagues.

Refinance my house.

Get my financial records in order.

Find a new dentist.

Find a new eye doctor.

Work with my coach on a new career plan.

Take my nieces and nephews to the zoo.

Read more for pleasure.

Sign up for some classes—maybe Spanish?

Hire an assistant at work.

Ted's Top-10 Procrastination List

After coming up with that extensive list, Ted made a list of the top ten things he wanted to tackle right away.

1. Clear out clutter from my home! Start with home office . . .

2. Clean up all files, including computer files (both at home and at work).

3. Deal with relationship with Tracy so that I can be supportive without feeling drained.

4. Change the nature of my friendships—stop spending time with people out of habit, DO pursue new friends who are more in tune with who I am now.

5. Eat better—less ice cream, more fruits and veggies. Really focus on this change so I lose a little weight and feel better.

6. Get more exercise—swim twice per week, walk three times.

7. Start letting go of the belief that I'm unlovable—do some serious reframing, affirmations, etc.

8. Stop being so judgmental!

9. Figure out new ways to meet possible friends or a long-term partner.

10. Find a new dentist and eye doctor.

Next, take a look at your habits. Getting rid of unhealthy, unhelpful habits can have a huge effect on your life. Consider getting rid of what Judith Wright in her book *There Must Be More Than This* calls "soft addictions." You know, the hours you spend in front of the TV, or the computer game where "just one game" turns into many—you find yourself, glassy-eyed, hours later, saying "I did it again!" What habits do YOU feel are really holding you back?

At the deepest level, examine your beliefs. Just as going from eliminating stuff to eliminating information is just a subtle variation, when it comes to people this examination happens at a much deeper level. Habits and beliefs in relation to people will never be so cut and dried as cleaning out your sock drawer.

Changing your beliefs is a deep process that occurs, when it occurs at all, over time and often with some outside help. But for now at least become aware of the beliefs that are holdovers from your past. The ones that hold you back. Self-limiting, self-defeating habits of mind that don't serve you. My mother told me as a child "You become what you think about." Who do you want to be?

Clearing the brush
MAKING YOUR LIST

*N*ow it's your turn! You've seen what Ted came up with. Hopefully, like Ted, you can see the value of clearing out the old to make room for the new. When I was sixteen, my mother gave me a poster for my bedroom with a Chinese proverb: "If you keep an open bough, the singing bird will come." It's time to clean out the clutter to create that open bough.

On a notepad, make a list now of **ALL** the things you can think of that are "hanging over your head." Look at your home, your workspace, your car, your relationships, and your emotional hang-ups. (Hint: relationships that are unsatisfying and need to end belong on this list. So do ones that need pursuing, for which you haven't made the time.) As Ted did, look at your information sources, your habits, and your beliefs, too. What's in the way of you being your best self? What really has to go? What needs to be fixed, changed, rearranged, or just plain eliminated? Ready, set, go! Write them all down.

YOUR TURN!
Your Top-10 Procrastination List

Now, reviewing your Clearing the Brush checklist, make a list of the top ten things you are putting off. You should start with the most urgent things—the things that are making you the most unhappy—and set a completion date goal:

Goal   Completion date

1.

2.

3.

4.

5.

6.

7.

8.

9.

10.

Taking Inventory

WHAT HAVE I LEARNED?

Congratulations! You just did a lot of work in looking at your current situation. I know some of it may have been painful. Take heart! This is your beginning point. It only gets better from here. Celebrate what's terrific in your life right now and realize that the not-so-terrific things can be put on notice. Change is coming!

To assess your progress "clearing out the brush," ask yourself the following questions:
• What was most challenging about doing this exercise?
• Did you see any patterns when you wrote about all the areas of your life and what needs to be cleared up?
• How did you react emotionally to being asked to make a list of things/people/ideas/beliefs to ELIMINATE?
• What do you think will be most difficult to clear out? If you are finding this process emotionally and physically draining, take heart that many have been on this path before you! Give yourself a pat on the back, indulge your favorite pastime, or give yourself a treat. You deserve it!

Dream It!
WHERE DO
I WANT TO GO?

In order to create the life you really want, you must first envision it in glorious detail. This part of the book gives you the tools and encourages you to dream a bigger dream. It is the futuristic, no-holds-barred part of creating your new life. The exercises in this part help move you "out of the box" of day-to-day reality and into the wide open space where you can picture clearly what you **REALLY** want.

What do I mean when I say "Dream a bigger dream"? I mean this:

- Instead of thinking "Maybe I could finish college going to school part time," go for what you **REALLY** want, "I'll complete my undergraduate studies, then get my Ph.D so I can teach at the University as I've longed to do."
- Rather than "I'd like to have a decent boyfriend," how about "I'd like to meet and marry the man of my dreams: kind, handsome, rich, whom I love…" Say **EXACTLY** what your heart desires.
- Or, the little dream could be "I'll join the writing group in town" when the bigger dream your heart is longing for is "I want to be a full-time writer, get paid well for my writing and have a book on the bestseller list."

Go for it! Dream a **BIGGER** dream! Seek out what you really want. Be bold. Be specific. And dream big.

I believe Robert Kennedy was quoting Aeschylus, the ancient Greek poet, when he said, "Some people see things as they are and ask 'Why?' I see things as they could be and ask 'Why not?'" Like Bobby Kennedy, I have always encouraged my clients to dream about how life **CAN** be.

You may agree that, if you're going to dream, you might as well dream big. But you may question whether the dreaming part accomplishes anything beyond entertaining you. To me, dreaming provides a key part of the foundation of your new life.

You see, quantum physicists are discovering what mystics and sages have always known—that "reality" as we know it is somewhat of an illusion. The world is more ephemeral and fluid than we might have imagined. We do know for sure that our lives as well as all material "realities" begin first as thoughts. In order to create the life of your dreams, first you must create it in your mind.

Why is this so important? Because whether or not you are conscious of it, your dreams and your imagination **WILL** create your future. There's power in doing this creative work consciously and with intention, rather than haphazardly letting life happen to you.

So, in Chapter 3 we'll explore your underlying values. When your goals are congruent with your values and your sense of life purpose, they are easier to achieve. Before settling upon a plan, you'll take a good look at your values as bedrock upon which your new life will be built.

Chapter 4 gives you the opportunity to look at your future self in a holistic way and envision **ALL** the dazzling possibilities. You'll draw up specific visions for each of our eight areas in the Wheel of Life.

In Part One you assessed your starting point. With Part Two, in a way, you're envisioning your ending point. What I know from years of coaching clients is that the most successful people are those with the clearest vision about what they want to accomplish and who they want to be. Do you really want to have a life you love? Then don't skip this part! Dream big! Be outrageous! But be diligent— write it all down. Actually, this part is really fun—let's get to it!

CHAPTER 3

Values are important. When values drive your dreams and actions, your life has flow and integrity. It has a sense of "being on purpose." Think of it this way: Before you met with a master architect to map out the home of your dreams, you'd first want to have a good idea of what you value. At twenty-seven, in a budding new career and with a full social life, you might value a home that is perfect for entertaining your friends, doesn't require a lot of boring maintenance, and maybe has room for a nursery as you envision marriage and a family. On the other hand, if you're part of a two-career family with three small kids, you may value a home with plenty of room for them to play . . . and a private master bedroom suite for your own sanity!

I BUILD MY HOUSE
upon this *Rock*

UNDERLYING VALUES

*B*efore you begin envisioning the life of your dreams, it's important to know what you value. Your values are the bedrock upon which your new life will be built.

That's what being your own life coach is all about: Start with a solid foundation, dream big, and then make it happen step by step.

Looking at Your Values

If I asked you, "What do you value? What's important to you?" chances are you'd rattle off a quick list of sure bets: family, love, friends, success, integrity, etc. And while the list might be accurate as far as it goes, I'd ask you if your life reflected those values. You see, the old maxim, "Actions speak louder than words," tells us something about our values.

*D*o you say that family is your number-one value but spend all your time doing other things? That's the problem I have with the popular exercise of asking you to choose your top ten values from a presented list. What are you likely to choose? You're probably not going to say, "I value avoiding tough situations," or, "I value being right no matter what!" Yet if our actions reveal what we value, well . . .

In this chapter, we're going to engage both the dreamer and the doer in you. Then the final page will let you come up with your own conclusions. You'll review what you learned about yourself and your values from looking at those you admire. And you'll see what your actual life says about what you value right now.

The structure of your new life will be laid upon this foundation—make it a strong one!

Whom Do You Admire?

WHY?

*H*ave you heard the phrase, "If you spot it, you've got it"? That's what this exercise is about. On page 52, I'm going to ask you to make a list of the people you admire most and then jot down what you admire about them.

I discovered how valuable this exercise could be when my business mentor stopped me as I was extolling his virtues. He asked me to tell him exactly what I admired about him. That was easy! When I finished my list he said, "Diane, everything you said about me is true about you. You would not be able to see these attributes in me if you didn't have them yourself."

For now, in terms of your own life, don't worry about whether or not you have any certain attribute—simply follow the instructions on the next page. And to make it easier, I'm giving you an example—my client Bill's list. I asked Bill to list the people he admired and jot down adjectives that describe what he admired about each of them. I asked him to think of people he knew personally as well as any celebrities or historical figures. Here's what Bill wrote:

BOB	MARY	DOUG	BENJAMIN FRANKLIN	TIGER WOODS
Flexible	Positive thinker	Committed to excellence	Versatile	Takes golf to highest level
Takes career risks	Strong	Intellectual	Intelligent	
Has strong faith in own capabilities	Committed to health	Positive	Curious	
Believes that "everything will be alright"	Unwavering	Good friend	Playful	
		Works out—values exercise	Inventive	
			Has a broad spectrum	

YOUR TURN!
YOUR "Dreamer" List: Values Clarification

*N*ow create your own list of ten people you admire and what you most admire about them. When you're finished, circle attributes that come up repeatedly, even if the wording is not exact (e.g., "good father," "good mother," and "loving aunt" might all equal "good family member"). In all of these exercises continue on a separate sheet if necessary.

Name   *Attributes*

_____

_____

_____

_____

_____

_____

_____

_____

_____

_____

_____

_____

_____

_____

_____

_____

_____

_____

_____

_____

_____

The "Doer" in You: Listmania!

$\mathcal{N}$ow we're going to engage the more analytical part of your brain to play detective with your current life. How you live tells you about what you value. We'll make lists of how you spend your time, what your information sources are (what you read/watch/surf on the Internet), and how you spend your money. We're going to move from an abstract idea—values—to actually observing what you value by how you spend your time and money and what information you seek.

Time

$\mathcal{T}$his exercise isn't theoretical, and it's going to take some effort. Get your calendar/date book out right now. I'd like for you to look over how you've spent your nonworking time during the past 30 days. List all of your activities and how much total time you've spent on each. If you have nothing noted for, say, last Thursday night, think about how you typically spend evenings at home. Is it watching TV? Just come up with your best guess for such nonworking hours in your calendar. What do you do most evenings? What have you done on the weekends over the past month or two? How much time do you spend working during "nonwork" hours? How much time on household chores? How much of your time is spent with family? Friends? Fun? Personal growth? Your spiritual life? Creativity? How about giving back to your community? Or learning? Where DOES the time go?

Jot down some answers in the space provided...

Activity   *Hours*

Money

*A*gain, we're going to look at FACTS. Look at your discretionary income. Where does it go? Track everything you spend for a week. With money, some values are going to be obvious, some less so. I spend a lot of money on books and magazines, and I value learning. I also spend a lot of money on coffee. Do I value coffee? Or is it that I value friendship and a lot of my money is spent having coffee with friends? What does that tell you about what you REALLY value? Even nondiscretionary expenses can give you clues. Most of us have to pay for housing and transportation. However, a young man may spend a lot on a flashy sports car and little on housing (living with parents). We can get some clues on what he values from this. When he's a young father he may spend on kids' clothes, etc. The point here is to pay attention to something you actually DO (spending money), rather than what you THINK your values are.

Spent where   *Amount*

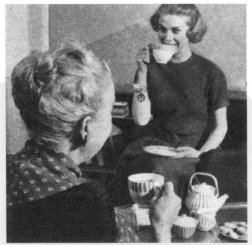

Information

*O*ur final list looks at the information you take in. What TV shows do you watch? What movies? What books have you read in the last month? What magazines do you read and which ones do you subscribe to? What do you have bookmarked on the Internet—what sites do you visit again and again? Pat watches HGTV, subscribes to *Victoria*, *Martha Stewart Living*, and *Better Homes and Gardens*. She's read two gardening books in the past month and has bookmarked several gardening sites on the Internet. What do you suppose Pat values? If you said gardening, you're half right. Pat values gardening as part of her overarching value of home. Now, to clarify what you really value, make your list. We've seen how you spend your time and your money. What do you do to feed your brain? The point here is to use what you learn from answering these questions as clues to lead us to what you actually value, rather than profess to value. You vote with your time, money, and attention. You'll have to look beneath the surface, especially with information. If you are a "news junkie," what is it that keeps you reading the paper, watching CNN, listening to the radio? Is it that you value being informed? Fitting in with the rest of the culture? Or is it just a habit? See what you can learn from looking at what information you seek on a regular basis.

Information source

_____

_____

_____

_____

_____

_____

_____

_____

_____

_____

_____

_____

_____

_____

_____

_____

_____

_____

_____

_____

_____

_____

_____

_____

Before building your dream house, or even consulting an architect, you'd probably look at possibilities. Maybe you'd go to a beautiful area and look at houses, or perhaps you'd study home design magazines. Based on this information, you'd soon be able to use one of your most powerful tools—your own imagination—to envision the house of your dreams.

DREAMING A BIGGER *Dream*

SITTING DOWN WITH THE MASTER ARCHITECT

*I*n this chapter, you're going to use your imagination and inner eye to envision your dream life. Close your eyes for a moment and picture your bedroom as a ten-year-old child. Can you see it? I see the lavender walls and the chenille bedspread, and oh, gosh, I see my sisters' dolls strewn around the floor. Can you "see" something from your past? Well, not only can you use the "inner eye," to remember your past, you'll use that same "inner eye" to envision the future you want to create.

Think about that for a moment. What if you could design a life that is absolutely perfect for you? A life in which your passions, interests, and gifts are all center stage. A life that hangs together with integrity, purpose, and meaning . . .

Here's the great news: You **CAN!** The first step is envisioning possibilities. As Goethe wrote, all bold action begins with a dream:

> **"Whatever you dream or think you can do, begin it. Boldness has magic and mystery in it."**

There's nothing mysterious about using your imagination to envision the future. You do it every day. But, if you're like most of us, your imaginative future is probably a scary place to be. How often do you find yourself picturing the worst possible outcome? This kind of active imagination is called worrying, and it never helps. Remember, what you focus on expands. Rather than imagining what can go wrong, put your energy into imagining what can go right. Doing so can change your life!

In this chapter, we will do some very specific and focused imagining. You will begin to create your new life by envisioning it in luscious detail.

Your Ideal Day

> Life is composed of days and moments. In this exercise, you will write about your ideal day. Here, the sky's the limit. Don't be bound by "reality" as you reach for the stars.

*F*irst take a few minutes to get calm and quiet. In your mind's eye, see yourself a year from today on a typical day in your ideal life—as you'd dream it to be. See yourself. How do you look? What are you doing? Who is with you? How do you spend your time? What do your surroundings look like? What kind of work are you doing? Make the picture in your mind as real as possible, filled with detail and passion. When you've spent enough time exploring this imaginary day, you'll want to write down the details so that you remember them.

To give you an idea of how this exercise might be done, here is what Jane wrote. Remember this is *her* dream, not yours. Read Jane's ideal day for a sense about the level of specificity you're looking for and about how you might "aim for the stars." Your own ideal day, though, may be very different from hers.

Jane's Ideal Day

After Tom, my husband, brings my coffee, I get up, and do some journaling. Then I do yoga for thirty minutes and have a great breakfast of fresh blueberries on cereal.

I do a few things around the house and then head across the street to the retreat center. In a typical month, we have at least one weekend retreat going on, and sometimes weeklong intensives. I check in with the retreat leaders to see what they need. On the first day of a new retreat, I speak to the participants, then follow this up with marketing, business development, and tasks around the office until lunchtime.

After lunch in the community center I hang out with my friends for a nice midday break before heading over to our school. I love to teach, and I've almost always got one or two courses. I teach my classes and then meet with students.

Dinner is either back at the community center or alone with Tom. My favorite evening is when Becky brings out her guitar, and we sit around a campfire and sing. I love that! In the winter, Tom and I read and cuddle by the fireplace. Toward the end of the evening, I check email, lounge around, and get ready to wind down. Before sleep, I say prayers of gratitude and write out ten things I'm most grateful for on this day. It's hard to stop with ten because I so love my life!

My Ideal Day

Okay, now it's your turn. Please take as much time as you need for this exercise. And DON'T be limited by any current constraints. The more specific you can be about your dream, the better. Details will help give your dream an authenticity you can feel and relish! Here are some questions to help you with this exercise:

🔥 *Where do you live? What does your space look like?*

🔥 *Are you alone? If not, who is with you?*

🔥 *What is the work you are doing? With whom?*

🔥 *What is bringing you joy and delight?*

🔥 *How do you see your own body?*

🔥 *What is nurturing your soul? Your spiritual life?*

_____

_____

_____

_____

_____

_____

_____

_____

_____

_____

_____

_____

_____

_____

_____

_____

My Future Self

*Thank you so much for coming
to celebrate my life with me
today. As I look around this room
at your cherished faces I am so
struck with wonder at how simple
life really is. All those earlier years
when I was striving for success,
money, and fame, how hard
I worked to improve myself!
It was decades before I realized
that love is what really matters.
And that relationships are far
more important than houses,
cars, and bank accounts
(though believe me, when you're
eighty, you WILL be glad you
put money aside!).*

*At the same time, I am proud
of what I've accomplished in the
world—the five books I've written,
two of which made the New York
Times best-seller list. I AM proud
of that achievement. I'm also very
proud of the business and
community I've created here with
the retreat center, the women's
health center, and our small but
thriving intentional community.
I know it sounds trite, but it's so
true—what I'm most proud of are
the relationships I've sustained in
my life. Though Tom's been dead
for six years, our long, happy
marriage is one of my greatest
treasures. And I'm proud of our
daughters—so dear to my heart.
I treasure the friendships I've
made—some have been with me
since childhood. Having people
like that in my life—now THAT is
an accomplishment!*

*A*nother way to access your bigger dreams is to visualize yourself as an older and wiser version of who you are and to seek advice from this Wise Elder. In the following exercise, you are invited to imagine that this Wise Elder has been living the ideal life you dream of and can help you get a clear picture of what this life looks like. You're about to attend your own eightieth birthday party, make a speech about your life, and hear what others have to say about you! When I recently attended my Aunt Marguerite's eightieth birthday party, I got to wondering: What is the legacy I'd like to leave? What would my eighty-year-old self want to tell me now?

Ask yourself these questions. In a moment, I'll ask you to write the speech you will give at YOUR eightieth birthday party. We're going to explore how you want your life to unfold from here by starting in the future. But before you begin, take a look at what Jane wrote:

On the following pages, you'll write a speech to be given by yourself, then tributes to be given by others, such as your spouse or best friend, your closest relative, and a person whose life you touched.

Your 80th Birthday Party Speech

Now it's your turn. On this page you will write the speech you will give at YOUR eightieth birthday party. But first, to prepare, ask yourself these questions:

🔥 *What sort of legacy would you want to leave behind?*

🔥 *Is there something concrete and specific you'd like to have accomplished?*

🔥 *What will it mean to have lived life well?*

🔥 *What's important to you?*

🔥 *Who has played a key role in your life and why?*

🔥 *Who would you LIKE to play a major role as you move forward?*

🔥 *What is likely to be in your obituary?*

🔥 *What will you be remembered for?*

_____

_____

_____

_____

_____

_____

_____

_____

_____

_____

_____

_____

I've known and loved Jane for four decades now. We felt so old when we met—all of forty we were! I've been so privileged to see Jane grow and mature and gain in wisdom and experience, while maintaining her youthful enthusiasm and curiosity. When we met, Jane was just beginning to think about what she would do next—the girls were all nearly grown, and she was restless. I remember when she realized, "I could write a book!" and how scared/enthused/stuck/enlivened she seemed to feel all at once. Writing that first book was quite a process, and I got to watch, not only the book take form, but a new Jane take form, too. I guess that's what I love best about Jane—she is always growing, always learning. And her love, warmth, and affection have been like the sunshine in my life. I treasure our long friendship.

<u>Your</u> 80th Birthday Party—what your spouse/ significant other and/or best friend had to say:

The aim of this exercise (and those on pages 64 and 65) is to assess how you want your future self to develop in relation to others. From the perspective of your eighty-year-old self, ask yourself:

- *How did you meet this person?*

- *What contributions have you made to his/her life?*

- *Why is she/he so important to you? Why do you suppose you are important to her/him?*

- *In what way do you annoy this person (and how could you change that?)*

- *What do you suppose this person finds most lovable about you?*

_____

_____

_____

_____

_____

_____

_____

_____

_____

_____

_____

_____

_____

_____

Your 80th Birthday Party—a close relative's speech:

Here are some things to consider before you write. Ask yourself:

🎉 *What is your relationship with this person?*

🎉 *What role did this person play in your childhood?*

🎉 *How has your relationship evolved over the years?*

🎉 *What are the best things to come out of this relationship?*

_____

_____

_____

_____

_____

_____

_____

_____

_____

_____

_____

_____

_____

What Jane's younger sister Denise had to say:

Well, Jane, you sure got all your orneriness out of your system early! After you quit pulling my hair when we were tiny tots, you've been my best friend and my protector ever since. When we were little kids I sort of looked up to you, but I don't think I knew you as a person. The true gift has been the friendship we've shared as adults. I feel like you've always been there for me. I love the way you ask me such great questions and then listen, really deeply listen to me. It really touched me that when you fell in love with Tom, whose daughters were quite young at the time, you called me constantly to ask for parenting advice. I love how sweet you have always been with my kids—they adore you, Jane, and rightly so. After Mom and Dad died, you have been the bedrock of our family.

I am so grateful that you are not only my older sister, but also my lifelong friend.

Jane, I had the great privilege of working for you for eighteen years at the retreat and learning centers you founded thirty years ago. Working for you totally changed my life! Before that time, I felt I had very little to offer the world. I didn't think I was smart enough and felt, prior to working for you, that I was lucky just to have a job to support my daughter.

Working for you in such close proximity, I was gifted with your incredible enthusiasm, vision, and love. You told me from the very first day that I could be and do whatever I wanted. But you didn't just tell me that; you helped me to 'dream a bigger dream' and then to give it wings! I felt my creativity, passion, and enthusiasm all come alive when I began working for you. Now, all these years later, I'm an acclaimed seminar leader, author, and teacher. I have made more money than I ever imagined possible. Better yet, I have a loving relationship with my partner and a daughter who makes me proud—not to mention my grandchildren. Jane, you opened the door and showed me the way. And you taught me about love just by being loving and being you. I love you, Jane! You changed my life.

<u>Your</u> 80th Birthday Party—a speech given by someone whose life you touched:

Reflect a bit before you write. This exercise involves imagining how you will touch the life of someone in the future. The speech is the story of your meeting with this imaginary person, told by that person at your eightieth birthday party. Ask yourself:

🐾 *Who is this person?*

🐾 *How did you meet?*

🐾 *Reflect on why she or he is in your life—not just how you met but why this person has remained in your life.*

🐾 *What did you do to impact their life? Why did you do it?*

🐾 *What role did this person play in YOUR life?*

_____

_____

_____

_____

_____

_____

_____

_____

_____

_____

_____

_____

_____

Extra Credit!

SEE the Big Picture by Making a Visionary Collage.

This exercise is fun! And it works! For you more visual, "right-brained" types, who are by now SO weary of lists, this exercise will get you jazzed up again!

For this exercise, get yourself a big piece of poster board and a supply of old magazines, photos, pens, crayons, glue, and scissors. What you are going to do is create a Visionary Collage: a picture of your heart's desires. Like a magazine spread, showing all aspects of life in an ideal home (think of *Better Homes and Gardens'* "House of the Year"), you're creating a colorful visual guide to your new life.

Choose pictures, photos, and words from anything that represents what you want in life. You might make your collage specific to one aspect (all pictures related to the type of home you want, or the kind of career you're envisioning, or your ideal mate). Or you might like to show the whole shebang.

For instance, my current collage has a section on spirituality with "Reflect on Your Blessings" cut out of the newspaper; "When you find your bliss, savor it" cut from a magazine; and a small reproduction of one of my favorite Matisse paintings from last year's calendar. It also has sections on friends, love, writing (The *New York Times* best-seller list!). I'd like a new laptop, so I included a picture of one I'd like. And in the center of the collage, the theme for this year: Season of Growth.

Get the picture? Your Visionary Collage should be uniquely about YOU, with pictures and words that show the universe exactly how you want your life to be. Hang your finished collage some place where you'll see it every day (mine is on my office door). It acts as a powerful stimulant to your subconscious. Try it and you'll see!

Taking Inventory

WHAT HAVE I LEARNED?

Well done! How does your life shape up? Did you access your dreams through words? Or did you find that the Visionary Collage really sparked your imagination and helped you to focus on your vision for the future? In the next chapter, we'll do more work on your dreams in a way that will really excite you about your future!

Use this page to write down any further reflections you may have after completing these exercises:
- What did you learn that could help you in your life now?
- Looking at yourself now through those Wise Elder eyes, how do you feel about yourself? How do you feel about your current life?
- What do you know now about the choices before you? Include any reflections you think may be helpful in shaping the years between now and the time when you'll really be a Wise Elder.

Make a list of what you would like to achieve during your lifetime.

_____

_____

_____

_____

_____

_____

_____

_____

_____

_____

_____

_____

_____

_____

_____

_____

_____

_____

_____

_____

Congratulations! You've done a LOT of work. You know where you're coming from, what your foundations are, and what you value most in life. And you've envisioned a wonderful future for yourself. Now we'll set some preliminary goals.

INTO THE FUTURE
Visioning
POSSIBILITIES

*T*he wonderful dreams and visions of where you want to go, what you want your life to be like are your "castles in the air." In the following chapters, you'll have the chance to refine these into a house you can really build. But for right now, let your imagination run wild. Refer to what you've learned about yourself in envisioning your ideal day and your Wise Elder self and by creating your Visionary Collage. Make no small plans! Don't let any gremlins or "buts" get in the way. It's just you and your dreams.

Remember the folks you met when we discussed your foundations in Chapter 1? Here we'll take a look at how each of them built upon their foundations by listing out their "castle" for the area in question. (You might want to go back and reread Chapter 1 to refresh your memory.)

On each page, you'll see my client's example, and then you can write about **YOUR** own "castles in the air." (But if a picture—drawn or cut from a magazine—or some other way of building your castle works better for you, go for it!)

Here are some of the types of questions you'll want to ask yourself to help clarify exactly what your dreams for each area of your life could be.

Let's start with one of my favorite questions:

"If you knew you could not fail, what would you do?" This is a great question to ask yourself as you look at **ALL** the areas of your life—if your success were guaranteed in work or money or romance or health what would you shoot for?

Fill in the blank for each area:

"In terms of my career, someday I'll…"

"In my financial future, I'd like…"

"When I have time what I'd like to share with friends and family is…"

"After I've accomplished what I want to at work, what I'd like to do for fun to reward myself is…"

"Once I've 'made it' I'd like to have a home…"

"When I get the time, I'd like to focus more on personal growth or my spiritual life by…"

"If I knew I was going to live a long time, I'd take better care of my health and well-being by…"

"I'd think I had died and gone to heaven if my romantic life included…"

Castles in the Air

CAREER

*K*en is the midlife career changer you met on page 16. Here are his top five career-related goals—his "castles in the air":

Ken's Castles in the Air for Career

1. Determine a clear career direction that works for me.

2. Working with like-minded people who share my interests.

3. Do work that totally engages my love of hands-on technical problem solving.

4. Do work that does not include the managerial (and political) aspects of my last job.

5. Have work I truly love that pays me enough for a comfortable life.

MONEY

*R*emember Dawn from page 18? She's a divorced, single mom in her thirties, currently working as a freelance graphic designer. Her financial situation, as she is recently divorced, is pretty shaky. Here's what she's aiming for:

Dawn's Castles in the Air for Money

1. Triple my income! (I really need to be financially self-sufficient.)

2. Start my own retirement savings.

3. Start a college savings plan for Daniel.

4. Reduce my mortgage payments.

5. Pay off all credit card debts and remain debt free.

Choose five dreams for each:

My Castles in the Air for Career

_____

_____

_____

_____

_____

_____

_____

My Castles in the Air for Money

_____

_____

_____

_____

_____

_____

_____

HEALTH & FITNESS

*A*nn, from page 20, is the forty-something executive on the go. She knows that her health HAS to be a top priority to allow her to work at her peak capacity. Ann has laid great health foundations, but, being ambitious, she wants even more!

Ann's Castles in the Air for Health & Fitness

1. Be in top physical shape, feeling 100 per cent trim, fit, and healthy.

2. Be more consistent in my exercise regime—go to gym or walk five days per week regularly.

3. Get a massage or play golf or tennis regularly—imperative for my mental, as well as physical, health.

4. Go to the migraine clinic and finally get to the root of that longstanding problem.

5. Meditate! (My coach has urged me to do this for years—I know she's right that it will really help settle me down.)

My Castles in the Air for Health & Fitness

_____

_____

_____

_____

_____

_____

_____

FRIENDS & FAMILY

*O*n page 22 you met Joe, the young software engineer from London whose life is rich and full with family and friends. Joe wants to maintain his strong family base as well as add a few other elements. As he shows, sometimes continuing the good you already have is a great goal!

Joe's Castles in the Air for Friends & Family

1. Be a top father to Elise and Ian and a top husband for Alicia.

2. Maintain closeness with my Mum and with my brother Mark.

3. Make more time to visit Alicia's family regularly.

4. Get together with the guys from the soccer club at least quarterly and make time for neighbors, such as Jack.

5. Come to the right relationship with Nigel—figure out how to have him in our lives without disruption.

My Castles in the Air for Friends & Family

_____

_____

_____

_____

_____

_____

_____

HOME

*Y*ou met Ted on page 24. In his thirties, he's a single gay man in a big house with lots of stuff. Clutter is definitely an issue for Ted, as you'll see with some of his goals:

Ted's Castles in the Air for Home

1. A clean, clutter-free home that feels spacious, airy, and light, with a home office that is tidy, organized, and up to date, and a clutter-free basement .

2. A new car.

3. A beautifully redone kitchen—a gourmet paradise!

4. A really cool couch for the living room.

5. A new leather jacket, if my favorite old one can't be repaired.

ROMANCE

*C*ourtney, age twenty-two (whom you met on page 26) is SO ready for romance! She loves her new life and her career, but she's really ready for Mr. Right to come along. Here's her dream:

Courtney's Castles in the Air for Romance

1. I'm looking for a wonderful, handsome, tall guy with integrity and character, who shares my interests (especially basketball, reading, and cats).

2. I need to love a man with whom I can share my deepest feelings, and who will share his with me.

3. I'd like a family, so a guy must want to be a dad.

4. I love to laugh and have fun—I want a partner who loves life as much as I do.

5. I'm pretty fit and active—a guy who'll run or roller-blade or go on ride bikes with me would be great.

My Castles in the Air for Home

_____

_____

_____

_____

_____

_____

_____

My Castles in the Air for Romance

_____

_____

_____

_____

_____

_____

_____

FUN & RECREATION

*M*ike, whom you met on page 28, is a busy thirty-something sales guy, husband, and dad. He's always busy serving others: his clients, his boss, his wife, his kids. "Mike time" is not on his calendar, and it needs to be.

Mike's Castles in the Air for Fun & Recreation

1. Take time for myself each week—even a little will help.

2. Once a month, have enough time to do something really fun—like going out to fly my remote control airplane.

3. Hang out with my friends more—go out for beers or pick-up basketball or bike rides.

4. Do things that are fun for me and for the family— like roller-blading with Danielle, family bike rides, low key family outings.

5. A REAL castle in the air—go fly fishing with my buddies for a week!

My Castles in the Air for Fun & Recreation

_____

_____

_____

_____

_____

_____

_____

PERSONAL GROWTH & SPIRITUAL DEVELOPMENT

*J*oanne, the university professor you met on page 30, is a fifty-seven-year-old widow looking for more meaning in her life now that she's on her own. She realizes that her personal growth and spiritual development is paramount right now.

Joanne's Castles in the Air for Personal Growth & Spiritual Development

1. Find a spiritual practice that REALLY works for me.

2. Attend a personal growth seminar at least three times a year.

3. Find a community of like-minded seekers—maybe take yoga classes.

4. Listen to the tapes from the spiritual retreat consider booking to go there in October.

5. Begin working with a spiritual mentor. I've wondered if a 12-step group could be a spiritual and emotional home for me.

My Castles in the Air for Personal Growth & Spiritual Development

_____

_____

_____

_____

_____

_____

_____

Taking Inventory

WHAT HAVE I LEARNED?

Was that fun? I hope you are now really excited about your future possibilities. You've had many opportunities to "dream a bigger dream" and envision a life you've longed for. Go back and reread what you've written. You've done a lot of work! Now it's time to take stock.

Ask yourself questions such as the following:
- Is it easy for you to envision the future? Is it easy to "dream big"? Why or why not?
- Were there any areas that were particularly challenging or particularly easy?
- Are there any dreams you've had consistently since you were a child? Have you always envisioned yourself in some type of future?
- Which areas were easiest for you to set goals in? Which were hardest? Which are you most excited about? Which are you most dubious about?

Don't be discouraged if you find it hard to imagine your dream and future. Look for stimulating ideas around you in magazines and in books. Talking to friends can help inspire you, too!

_____

_____

_____

_____

_____

_____

_____

_____

_____

_____

_____

_____

_____

_____

_____

_____

_____

PART 3

Plan It!

HOW DO I GET THERE?

> **"If you have built castles in the air, your work need not be lost; that is where they should be. Now put foundations under them."**
>
> —*Henry David Thoreau*

*M*y friend Bill says, "Plan your work and work your plan." He's right! Whether you're heading for Paris or Pittsburgh, having a roadmap will make the journey easier, clearer, and more enjoyable.

This part will help you to turn the broad-stroke dreams you came up with in Part Two into measurable, achievable goals.

In Chapter 6, you'll focus on setting goals that say **"I'M SMART"**; that is, my goals have **I**nner **M**otivation, **S**pecificity, **M**easurability, and **A**ttainability, with **R**esources and a **T**imetable.

In Chapter 7, you'll map those specific goals into yearly, quarterly, monthly, and weekly targets. Businesses do this type of planning all the time to stay on track. Why shouldn't you have the benefit of the same care and attention for yourself? Business leaders know, planning is a key element in financial success. And your planning is about **MORE** than financial success (though that well may be a goal and an outcome)—it is about the success of your life and your dreams.

This part is the bridge from your dreams to their manifestation, so do it well!

CHAPTER 6

Now you'll set specific, measurable goals. You may not need or want to set goals for the year ahead in all areas. Sometimes it's a work year or a family year or a fix-up-your-house year, as you may want to focus heavily on one area of your life.

THE drawing *Board*

CREATING THE BLUEPRINT

*S*ometimes people do want to make incremental changes across the board—setting achievable goals in all the areas we've covered. Sometimes these goals are somewhat related, sometimes not. Just as often people have particular areas of focus—perhaps wanting to make positive career changes and simultaneously spiff up their home—but choosing **NOT** to focus for now on, say, Heath & Fitness. The point here is that we will cover how to go about setting meaningful goals, regardless of their scope. You can set goals across the board or in just one area of your life.

How do you know how to set goals or how to prioritize? Sometimes it's obvious. If you've lost your job and you're not independently wealthy, focusing on career should be fairly self-evident. At other times you may just feel like nothing is wrong, but nothing is exactly right either—you want life to be better all the way around. However, don't take on more than you can handle.

If you're not clear about where your goals need to be, go back to the Wheel of Life on page 15 and see which areas seem to call for the most focus.

Getting Smart

Once, you're clear about what areas you'll set goals in, I'm going to challenge you to set S T R E T C H goals for yourself. Ask yourself to do just a bit more than you think you can. Don't set yourself up for failure by asking yourself to do the impossible, but don't wimp out here either! In fact, before you start, you may want to stand up and physically stretch to set the tone. Then, set goals that say I'M SMART:

Inner Motivation—My goals reflect my values.
Specificity—They are clearly defined and detailed.
Measurability—There are benchmarks; I'll know when I've reached them.
Attainability—My goals are possible for me to accomplish.
Resources—I take responsibility and have what I need.
Timetable—I have definite deadlines for achievement.

Before you set your own goals, let's see how this **I'M SMART** approach works on a specific goal Jane set and how Lisa got more focused.

I'M SMART!
Jane's Case Study

Goal for year: Buy a new car that is stylish and dependable.

Inner Motivation—It really is time to get a new car. A reliable car means I could also look for a job elsewhere.

Specificity—I want to get a slightly used car that has low mileage, is fuel-efficient, can haul stuff around but doesn't look stodgy. And if I could find a red one that would be very cool. And I want to spend $16,000 or less.

Measurability—I'd like to have the car in my garage within three months so I can measure the timeframe (including time to research, shop, etc.).

Attainability—I need to plan it and save money and schedule it, but it IS do-able.

Resources—I take responsibility and I have the time, money, and energy to do this. Specifically, I have $8000 in my money market account and I'm willing to take on an $8000 car loan. I've set aside some time over the next six weeks to find one. And I'm excited about it—so I have lots of energy for this.

Timetable—Research thoroughly: two weeks, shop for two to four weeks, then some time to "haggle." I believe I can accomplish this in two months. But I commit to having this totally completed within three months.

Remember Lisa from Chapter 1? Lisa's in her mid-thirties, and eager to get more focused. She knew she wanted to meet the man of her dreams, have a more meaningful career, a new car, and a house. She came up with these goals for each of the eight areas of her life for the year ahead.

I'M SMART!

Lisa's Case Study

Goals for the year:

Career
Find a new job in Chicago at the end of Month 3.

Money
Fund the move to Chicago and Ph.D. program (need $18,000).

Health & Fitness
FINALLY lose that final 15 lbs (7 kilos)!

Friends & Family
Take out my niece Julia regularly. Expand my social circle.

Home
Redecorate new place.

Romance
Be dating someone seriously by the end of Month 6.

Fun & Recreation
Try one new restaurant a month Actually PLAY my piano!

Personal Growth & Spiritual Development
Begin Ph.D. program in psychology.

Your Goals for the Year Ahead

*N*ow, set your own area goals that you would like to accomplish in the next twelve months. We'll work back and set interim goals shortly. But for now, lay out how you want your life to be in each area and what the goals are to get you there. This is the heart of the planning exercise, so give it your time and full attention.

Be sure to do the **I'M SMART** check for each goal first. Ask yourself:

*1. Do I have the **I**nner **M**otivation to do what it takes to achieve this?*

*2. Is the goal **S**pecific? Do I need to make it clearer?*

*3. Is it **M**easurable? How will I know when I've reached it?*

*4. Is it **A**ttainable? (Stretch big, but make sure you give yourself the opportunity to succeed by choosing doable goals.)*

*5. Do I have the **R**esources I need to achieve this goal?*

*6. Have I set this goal into a definite **T**imetable?*

Remember, if you choose to you can set a goal (or goals) for each area. Or not! If you need more space to write, you can continue on a separate sheet of paper.

Career:

_____
_____
_____
_____
_____

Money:

_____
_____
_____
_____
_____

Health & Fitness:

_____
_____
_____
_____
_____

Friends & Family:

_____
_____
_____
_____
_____

Home:

_____
_____
_____
_____
_____

Romance:

_____
_____
_____
_____
_____

Fun & Recreation:

_____
_____
_____
_____
_____

**Personal Growth &
Spiritual Development:**

_____
_____
_____
_____

CHAPTER 7

Now it's time to figure out exactly how you will achieve your goals. Like a general contractor, you'll draw up a schedule to map out what needs to be done to make your dream a reality. The tools in this chapter will help you create a quarterly plan and teach you ways to measure your progress against the schedule you've set for yourself.

SCHEDULES

Turning a *Vision*

INTO A
STEP-BY-STEP PLAN

*Y*ou will be setting your goals as you go along: Don't sit down in Month 1 and map out goals for the entire year; rather, before each quarter begins map out that particular three months. We're going to next talk about the importance of measuring your progress, and how these quarterly goals fit into that.

And then I'll ask you to look at the yearly goals you set on page 85. You're going to first see an example of Lisa's quarterly goals and then set some of your own. You may also want to include specific tasks by quarter related to things you wish to eliminate, from

Clearing the Brush on page 38 ("donated old computer to charity," or "cleared out all old papers from filing cabinets," or "getting off those e-lists I no longer read.").

By getting specific—having written plans and a means to measure your progress—you are virtually ensuring success.

So let's get going!

Measuring Progress

*T*here are two ways you will measure the progress of your yearly goals. One involves your heart; the other, your head. On the heart level, I urge you to check in with yourself periodically and see if the goals you set as you began this process still resonate with you. Consistency and "staying the course" are a key part of success. You've probably heard, though, of the danger of "climbing the ladder of success, only to find it's been placed against the wrong wall." Periodically making sure that your goals are still appropriate for you is a wise part of measuring your progress. It allows you to make midcourse corrections.

But once you know your goals are right for you, keep on top of them! This is where your head, as well as your heart, gets into the act. In Chapter 8, we'll talk about further refining your objectives and mapping out, not just yearly and quarterly goals, but monthly, weekly, and daily ones as well. For now, I encourage you to do what I do with my coaching clients: Have update meetings with yourself.

Going over your goals

At the end of each quarter, schedule some time to go over your goals for the previous quarter and set new ones for the quarter ahead. About two weeks before the quarter ends is a good time for this exercise.

During your scheduled time, take out your yearly goals and your quarterly goals and your calendar. Review your progress. How did you do? Are you on track? If yes, congratulate yourself and take some time to savor your achievements before you rush headlong into setting the next batch of goals.

If you're not on track, can you find out what happened? We may not make as much progress as we'd like for many different reasons.

Maybe your goals shifted just slightly, but enough to throw you off. Or maybe unexpected big events came your way: not the usual flurry of life, but something more substantial—a new job, a death in the family, a surprise romance. Or perhaps external events over which you have no control knocked your well-laid plans out of orbit (e.g., your company just announced pay CUTS for everyone across the board, and so your financial goals are suddenly impacted).

But maybe it's not the case that any such external force impacted your progress. Maybe you're just not quite where you want to be. That's okay—don't waste your time and emotional energy beating up yourself. Just figure out what happened, what you want to have happen instead, and regroup. Then, once you've recapped the quarter that just passed, set goals for the next quarter.

By first checking inside—are these still goals that make my heart sing?—and then using your head to measure your current progress, you set yourself up to make meaningful goals for the next quarter. If you make this practice a habit, quarter by quarter, you'll move closer toward the life you really want throughout the year.

I'm picturing the big thermometer signs you sometimes see with fund-raising efforts. Imagine a large thermometer with numbers on the left-hand side showing amounts of money to be raised. As each benchmark is reached ($25,000, $50,000, $75,000, $100,000), the thermometer is filled in.

Your quarterly check-ups can provide you that same type of progress report.

So is the temperature getting any warmer?

Quarter 1
Your Goals

hile some yearly goals are easy to dissect (to save $10,000 this year, save $2500 this quarter), most quarterly goal-setting is more intuitive than scientific. If your goal is to get a new job (as is Lisa's—see her goals listed to the right), what do you need to do in the next three months? As you'll see, Lisa had three major tasks to focus on in the first quarter to get her toward her career goal of finding a new job. For each yearly goal you've set, think about what you need to do in the next three months to move you forward enough to reach this goal on time. Think of two or three achievable goals.

Quarter 1—YOUR Goals

Now **YOU** set your goals for the first quarter of the year, or for the next three months if you're starting midyear. Before beginning, ask yourself questions like this:

- What do I need to do in the next three months to move forward with this goal?
- Is there research that needs to be done prior to moving into action?
- Who do I need help from to move this forward?
- Do I need to "clear the brush" in any way before moving forward?
- Am I making this too hard? Can I simplify my approach?

Remember, if you choose to you can set a goal (or goals) for each area. Or not!

Lisa's Goals for Quarter 1

Career
Update résumé.
Contact everyone I know in Chicago and tell them I'm looking for a job.
Continue to search job boards.

Money
Have garage sale.
Cut spending by $25 a week

Health & Fitness
Walk for fitness three times a week.
Lose at least 6 lbs (3 kilos).

Friends & Family
Call my niece (Julia) twice a month.
Have dinner party in Month 2.

Home
Clear closets! Go through all books and CDs for garage sale.
Tackle at least one filing cabinet.

Romance
Nothing yet—I want to meet a guy in Chicago, not San Diego.

Fun & Recreation
Book up to go to that new cool Thai restaurant.
At least play my piano ONCE.

Personal Growth & Spiritual Development
Complete Ph.D. application process.
Try meditating again.

Career
Specific 3-Month Goal(s):

_____

_____

_____

_____

_____

Money
Specific 3-Month Goal(s):

_____

_____

_____

_____

_____

Health & Fitness
Specific 3-Month Goal(s):

_____

_____

_____

_____

_____

Friends & Family
Specific 3-Month Goal(s):

_____

_____

_____

_____

_____

Home
Specific 3-Month Goal(s):

_____

_____

_____

_____

_____

Romance
Specific 3-Month Goal(s):

_____

_____

_____

_____

_____

Fun & Recreation
Specific 3-Month Goal(s):

_____

_____

_____

_____

_____

Personal Growth &
Spiritual Development
Specific 3-Month Goal(s):

_____

_____

_____

_____

Quarter 2
Your Goals

Before setting your goals for the next quarter, take a moment to review your yearly goals and also to assess how you did in the quarter that just passed. This is a great time to "regroup." Have any of your goals changed? Has your approach towards achieving them changed now that you've had three months to move toward your dreams? What was most effective last quarter? What will you do differently now? In what areas are you behind? On track? Ahead?

Quarter 2—YOUR Goals

Have a look at Lisa's goals for the second quarter (based on her yearly goals, shown on page 83). When you're ready, set your goals for the second quarter (the next three months).

Lisa's Goals for Quarter 2

Career
Look for work in Chicago.
Join job-leads group as soon as I get to Chicago.

Money
Use severance package to pay for move to Chicago.
Save money while staying short-term with my friend Suzanne.

Health & Fitness
Lose another 4 lbs (2 kilos).
Take up roller-blading.

Friends & Family
Once I'm in Chicago, take Julia to Lincoln Park Zoo.
Hook up with Chicago friends again!

Home
Clear out clutter before the move to Chicago.
Move to Chicago!

Romance
Get friends to help set up blind dates to find Mr. Right.

Fun & Recreation
Blues bars, out for pizza, the nightlife scene—can hardly wait!

Personal Growth & Spiritual Development
Start journaling again (in order to create a quiet space for myself).

Career
Specific 3-Month Goal(s):

_____

_____

_____

_____

_____

Money
Specific 3-Month Goal(s):

_____

_____

_____

_____

_____

Health & Fitness
Specific 3-Month Goal(s):

_____

_____

_____

_____

_____

Friends & Family
Specific 3-Month Goal(s):

_____

_____

_____

_____

_____

Home
Specific 3-Month Goal(s):

_____

_____

_____

_____

_____

Romance
Specific 3-Month Goal(s):

_____

_____

_____

_____

_____

Fun & Recreation
Specific 3-Month Goal(s):

_____

_____

_____

_____

_____

Personal Growth &
Spiritual Development
Specific 3-Month Goal(s):

_____

_____

_____

_____

Quarter 3
Your Goals

O nce again, it's helpful to review your yearly goals and your progress to date. Now that you've got six months of learning to draw upon, it should be fairly easy to set this quarter's goals.

Quarter 3—YOUR goals

Ask yourself things like:

- How am I feeling now that I'm six months into this process?
- What goals have I already completed and achieved?
- Did I celebrate my accomplishments?
- What has contributed most to my success to date?
- Who or what do I need to add to my life this quarter to achieve the next round of goals?
- Is there a particular area I really want to emphasize in the next three months? If so, what am I willing to let up on a bit so I can surge forward in the focus area?
- How has my focus changed since I began this process six months ago?
- And, of course, what specifically do I need to do in each goal area during the next three months to stay on track towards success?

Have a look at Lisa's goals for the third quarter and then **YOU** set your goals for the next three months.

Lisa's Goals for Quarter 3

Career
Found a great job that will work with my Ph.D. program, so my main goal is to settle in.

Money
Secure a student loan to help when I start grad school.

Health & Fitness
Still need to lose one final pound (0.5 kilo) to meet my goal. Keep exercising.

Friends & Family
Make Julia's birthday memorable! Be bridesmaid at Sue's wedding.

Home
Get an apartment of my own. Move into it! And decorate.

Romance
Check out social activities. Consider signing up for "It's Just Lunch" dating service.

Fun & Recreation
Barter piano lessons in return for cooking for my friend Alex.

Personal Growth & Spiritual Development
Keep journaling. Start Ph.D. program. Sign up for personal growth workshop.

Career
Specific 3-Month Goal(s):

_____

_____

_____

_____

_____

Money
Specific 3-Month Goal(s):

_____

_____

_____

_____

_____

Health & Fitness
Specific 3-Month Goal(s):

_____

_____

_____

_____

_____

Friends & Family
Specific 3-Month Goal(s):

_____

_____

_____

_____

_____

Home
Specific 3-Month Goal(s):

_____

_____

_____

_____

_____

Romance
Specific 3-Month Goal(s):

_____

_____

_____

_____

_____

Fun & Recreation
Specific 3-Month Goal(s):

_____

_____

_____

_____

_____

**Personal Growth &
Spiritual Development**
Specific 3-Month Goal(s):

_____

_____

_____

_____

_____

Quarter 4
Your Goals

ow! If you're at this point you have completed nine months of goal-setting. By now some of your goals have been achieved. And, if you're like most of us, several other goals have either been abandoned or have changed. You probably still have some goals that you want to complete in the next three months, though. This is a great time to take stock of your overall goals, look at where you've come in the past nine months, and prepare for your final quarter of this year. Perhaps now you can see next year's goals and dreams on the horizon, too. It's not "cheating" to add to your goal list as you begin each quarter—just make sure that your overall plan fits with your overarching ideals and values. Ask yourself the types of questions that you have been asking for the past three quarters. Things like:

- How am I doing overall?
- Am I still energized by these goals or have I gotten on to a treadmill? If it feels like a rut, what do I need to change?
- What do I need to do in the next three months to achieve these goals?
- What have I learned in the last quarter?
- Am I pleased overall with my progress? If not, what do I need to change? If yes, how have I celebrated my successes?

When you've reflected and adjusted your goals accordingly and had a look at Lisa's goals for the fourth quarter (based on her yearly goals, shown on page 83), choose your goals for the fourth quarter (the next three months).

Lisa's Goals for Quarter 4

Career
Things are going well.

Money
Put aside money for computer.

Health & Fitness
Hurrah! Keep off the 10 lbs (5 kilos) I have lost
Get 8 hours sleep every night.
Eat five fruits/veggies per day.

Friends & Family
Go see Julia perform in her high school play.
Visit family over the vacation.

Home
Keep my desk tidier.
Get new flannel sheets—I forgot how cold Chicago is.

Romance
Keep dating Tom—an exciting new relationship.

Fun & Recreation
Go ice-skating at Millennium Park with Tom and my old pals.
Life is very full—let piano go?

Personal Growth & Spiritual Development
Keep up with studies in Ph.D. program.
Keep journaling.
Continue with workshop.

Career
Specific 3-Month Goal(s):

_____

_____

_____

_____

_____

Money
Specific 3-Month Goal(s):

_____

_____

_____

_____

_____

Health & Fitness
Specific 3-Month Goal(s):

_____

_____

_____

_____

_____

Friends & Family
Specific 3-Month Goal(s):

_____

_____

_____

_____

_____

Romance
Specific 3-Month Goal(s):

_____

_____

_____

_____

_____

Romance
Specific 3-Month Goal(s):

_____

_____

_____

_____

_____

Fun & Recreation
Specific 3-Month Goal(s):

_____

_____

_____

_____

_____

Personal Growth &
Spiritual Development
Specific 3-Month Goal(s):

_____

_____

_____

_____

Taking Inventory

WHAT HAVE I LEARNED?

Wow! That was really some work you just did. In Part Two, you used your right brain, the part that is more visual, to create an imagined future. Then in Part Three, you used your left brain, the analytical and more detail-oriented part, to move from the world of dreaming and visioning into the realm of manifestation. Part Three provided the bridge between your dreams and their actualization in the form of specific goals, timeframes, and schedules.

Before you go on, use this page to summarize your plans.
Ask yourself questions like:
- What feelings did this part of the book evoke?
- Are you excited about the detailed planning you just did? Nervous?
- Are you not sure you can pull it off?
- Are you feeling trapped by the specificity?

Write about the issues that came up for you as you did this planning.
Don't worry if your reactions feel trivial or extreme: writing them
down will help you to focus on issues that are important for you to
deal with.

PART **4**

Do It!

HOW DO I GET INTO ACTION?

*C*ongratulations! Your dream has been turned into a set of achievable plans. This part moves you into realizing them It is filled with secrets that successful life builders use to get into—and stay in—action.

Sometimes smart people fail even though they have great vision. They seem able to map out a plan, but yet still fail to make it a reality. That doesn't have to happen to you. Having good time-management skills, good habits to help you implement your plan, and good relationships to support you in your quest are all secret tools that successful people know and use. You can, too!

In Chapter 8, you'll learn how to go from quarterly plans to specific monthly, weekly, and daily goals.

Then, in Chapter 9, you'll explore habits. We all have habits and routines, conscious or unconscious. In this chapter, you'll focus on establishing helpful habits to enhance your day-to-day life.

As a coach, I know how crucial support is for successful, energetic, creative people. The lone hero has always been a myth. Now, more than ever, as we move into a more collaborative century, it is essential that you have good support as you progress toward your dreams. And that's what we'll explore in Chapter 10.

"Action may not always bring happiness; but there is no happiness without action."

—Benjamin Disraeli

Dreamers dream. Successful people also plan and implement. This chapter gets you further across the bridge between your dreams of a better life and actually living there.

JUST *Do It!*

SECRETS OF A MASTER BUILDER

*T*his is the chapter that will teach you to take your yearly and quarterly goals and create monthly, weekly, and then daily goals.

You know all the clichés that speak to this process:

- "A journey of a thousand miles begins with one step."
- "How do you eat an elephant? One bite at a time."
- "Just do the next right thing."

In my successful fifteen-year corporate career, I became an expert project manager. I mapped out large projects, allocating people and resources over the course of time to create systems, software, or processes.

But you don't have to be a project manager to accomplish the same result. This chapter will lead you through determining what you need to do this month, this week, today—in the next hour—to move you toward goals that may feel large, far away, or even unachievable.

Just <u>DO</u> It!

Let's anchor your action in your dreams, goals, hopes, values, and ideals. Revisit, for a moment, your Visionary Collage, your values, your yearly goals, and, finally, the quarterly goals you set for yourself on page 91. Please, do yourself a favor. Don't just read the previous sentence. Actually take the time to LOOK at your collage and reread what you wrote.

N ow that you've reminded yourself of what it is that you **REALLY** want, it's time to get more concrete. For this chapter you will need:

1. **Your Visionary Collage**
2. **Your quarterly goals**
3. **Your calendar**
4. **Your willingness to do things differently**

Maybe you're the kind of person who thrives on structure. I know you. You set plans for yourself, draw up a schedule, and then do it.

No? Are you the kind of person who is "all over the map," always rushing about, constantly busy, tired, and stressed—but not productive? Does that sound more familiar?

Or, like most of my clients and friends, and indeed myself—are you sort of a combination of the two? You keep a calendar, you set goals, and you actually achieve some, too. But you have that nagging feeling that things could be better. You're ready to do it differently in order to create the life you really want to be living.

The tools in these next three chapters will show you how to get there. Over the next six pages, you will walk through a process to help you in your planning. Each part of the process will first have

an example, based on Lisa's goals from Chapter 7, followed by room for you to write your goals for the month, week, or day.

You'll take your list of quarterly goals (from page 91) and create specific subgoals for each of the next three months. For now, you'll start with Month 1. Once you have this month's goals delineated, you'll move on to set goals for this week that will help you achieve the month's goals.

Finally, you'll see what **REALLY** makes a difference in this part of your work: going from yearly/quarterly/monthly/weekly goals to **DAILY PLANS** that are **WRITTEN IN TO YOUR CALENDAR**. This final part of Chapter 8 is the secret ingredient that can catapult you to success! You don't just set a goal; you concretely assign time to make it happen.

Let's move into action on this now!

MONTHLY goals

Your Goals

So you've got your collage, your yearly goals, and even your quarterly goals in front of you. How do you move from that level of granularity to knowing what you need to do in the next month to move you toward making your vision a planned reality?

For some goals, this is easy. If you have a very specific, numerical goal ("save $1200") you may be able to simply divide the quarterly goal by three, and voilà! your monthly goal is in front of you ("save $400 this month"). Other goals also lend themselves to a fairly analytical solution. If one of your goals is to spend more time with your children, you can look at this month's calendar and plan in advance ("Take the kids to the zoo on June 1.").

Other goals aren't so cut and dried. You know you want to deepen more spiritually and focus on personal growth—but how are you going to translate that into moving forward **THIS MONTH** so you can achieve your quarterly, yearly, and longterm goals?

Some of this requires your intuition and focus more than your calendar and will-power. Focus matters. So, for goals that seem more nebulous, I'd ask you to consider, "How can I focus on this area of my life? What action, attitude, introspection or openness will lead me forward this month?" The important part in monthly planning is to focus on your quarterly goals and look for **"I'M SMART"** ways to move yourself toward them this quarter.

Lisa's Goals for Month 1

In this example, some goals are one-time events, others involve habits. Most relate directly to Lisa's quarterly goals, but there's spontaneity, too.

Career
Update my existing résumé.
Send email to all my friends in Chicago about job search.

Money
Cut spending by $25 a week.

Health & Fitness
Walk three times a week.
Make dentist appointment.

Friends & Family
Call Julia (niece) twice a month.
Go out to dinner with Kristi.

Home
Clear closets.
Replace bathroom towels in sale.

Romance
Go with Laurie to that "speed dating" thing.

Fun & Recreation
Go to that new cool Thai place.

Personal Growth & Spiritual Development
Join study group focusing on Julia Mossbridge's book "Unfolding," about the "soul's work."

<u>YOUR</u> Monthly Goals

*O*kay, now it's your turn. You may want to make a copy of this page so you can set goals each month as you work through the year. Remember, though I'd encourage you to focus on one to three items in each category, it's okay to have some areas with more or fewer goals.

Area   Goals For This Month

Career

_____

_____

Money

_____

_____

Health & Fitness

_____

_____

Friends & Family

_____

_____

Home

_____

_____

Romance

_____

_____

Fun & Recreation

_____

_____

Personal Growth & Spiritual Development

_____

_____

WEEKLY goals
Your Goals

Your Goals

Lisa's Goals for Second Week in Month 1

As you look at Lisa's weekly goals, you'll see they relate to her monthly (and thus quarterly and yearly) goals.

Career
Follow up with lead Jennifer sent me for a job at Sears.

Money
Save $25 by not going out to lunch this week.

Health & Fitness
Walk with walking partners on Wednesday.

Friends & Family
Call Julia.
Go out to dinner with Kristi.

Home
Clear out closets.
Put giveaway stuff in bags to donate to charity.

Romance
Nothing.

Fun & Recreation
Go to party at Marcia's.
Go to introductory step class at fitness center near my office.

Personal Growth & Spiritual Development
Read first chapter of Julia Mossbridge's book.

reat! So now you've gone from a high level ideal, to specific goals for the year and quarter ahead, to having very clear goals for the next month. What's next? Now you'll go from Monthly goals to what you're going to accomplish to move you toward your vision **THIS WEEK**.

Using the same methodology and applying it now to a tighter timeframe, simply look at your monthly goals and map out first **WHAT** you plan to do this week so that you'll have achieved what you set you out to by month's end. And then look at **WHEN** you want to do that.

I encourage clients to have a specific "Weekly Goal-Setting" time. For many of us it's Sunday afternoon or evening, or it's Monday morning. Pick a time that works for you and stick to it. Get used to looking at your monthly goals and planning out the week ahead. When planning the *what*, roughly pencil in the *when*, if applicable. So "take kids to the zoo" gets mapped into next Saturday. If it happens on Sunday instead, that's okay—but get it on the schedule, at least in some tentative way.

<u>YOUR</u> Weekly Goals

*O*kay, now it's your turn. You may want to make a copy of this page so you can set goals each week.

Area   **Goals For This Week**

Career

_____

_____

Money

_____

_____

Health & Fitness

_____

_____

Friends & Family

_____

_____

Home

_____

_____

Romance

_____

_____

Fun & Recreation

_____

_____

Personal Growth & Spiritual Development

_____

_____

DAILY planning *Your Goals*

Now, here comes the secret to success: put these weekly goals into your calendar! Life is swift and things change, so when the week is done, you may find that the task you assigned yourself for Tuesday actually got done two days earlier on Sunday—or even three days later on Friday—but by setting specific timeframes for each task you're far more likely to get them done. Now you are taking charge of your life and your time, instead of leaving things to chance.

For many of us, it will make sense to have more structure during the work week, less on the weekends. If being **TOO** structured is likely to make you feel cramped and lead to rebellion, then use a broader brush for this part of planning. But, whatever your style is, you need to **PLAN**. Yes, leave room for spontaneity, but have a roadmap, a clear focus that will move you toward your desires.

Do you see how this moves you forward toward your ideal life? You start with your vision, turn it into a broad set of goals, and set specific plans for the year ahead. Then it becomes like a puzzle. To get to the year's goals, what must I do this month? To achieve all I've mapped out for the month, what needs to be done this week? If I'm going to make my plan for the week, what's on tap today?

Lisa's Diary for Monday

7–7:30 A.M. Walk with Jack and Sally.

9–10 Go to staff meeting.

10–12 Meet with consulting company about outsourcing department functions.

12–1 P.M. Lunch—eat at desk (save $s!).

1:30–3 "Free time"—call Mary and schedule performance review, catch up on email, work on compensation study report.

3–4 Attend benefits group meeting.

4–5 Check email, voice mail; call legal to set up appointment to discuss a colleague's retirement.

7:30 Clean out closets! Talk to Jill on the phone while I'm at it.

9:00 Internet time! Get Dr. Sears and Dr. Glasgow's addresses, check out the news, and hang out for a bit in chat room.

<u>YOUR</u> Daily Plan

You're smart. You understand what I'm talking about. You probably even buy into the usefulness of this approach. What I've found is that this is the **CRUCIAL** juncture in your journey to success. This step, right here, is where it either comes together or falls apart. It comes together when you stop reading this book, get your weekly list (you **DID** do one, back on page 109, didn't you?) and your calendar and map out the week ahead. Then, having planned your work, you simply work your plan. Things fall apart in a few different ways:

You think, "Well, alright then, this is a great approach for other people, but it will never work for me, because . . ."

You **INTEND** to get started, but in a few minutes, or a few hours, or next week . . .

You write things in your calendar, diligently, and then never look at it again.

Action leads to satisfaction. Dreamers dream; successful people plan. And then they work on their plans. Who do you want to be?

Tasks to Accomplish on Day 1 of Plan

Morning:

_____

_____

_____

_____

Afternoon:

_____

_____

_____

_____

Evening:

_____

_____

_____

_____

Be sure to write down a schedule as above for each day.

Put Yourself First

GETTING ON YOUR OWN CALENDAR

Where does spontaneity fit into all of this planning? Are we to become robots? Not at all! If you're like me, having too tight a tether will create an immediate rebellion! So it's important to have blocks of "free time'" (at least, time that is not scheduled) in your calendar. These periods can be used in many ways. Most importantly, we all need down time, so some of them will be that. Some will be helpful when you have taken advantage of an unexpected opportunity and so have not focused on what you had planned to do. For instance, your neighbor spontaneously invites you to an impromptu gathering that sounds like a lot of fun—and it's this Wednesday. Wednesday, as it turns out, was when you were finally going to clean your office. But no problem, you have a few hours free on Saturday morning. You can clean the office then.

Realistically, you probably won't get **EVERYTHING** on your list done. But I can guarantee that if you use this system to put yourself first, you will get **LOTS** more done than you used to!

I'd also like to emphasize the importance of putting self-care activities on your calendar. I don't mean your doctor and dentist appointments, though they need to be there, too (and you **DO** get regular checkups, right?). Instead, I'm referring to those nurturing-the-soul activities that help you do all that you do by regularly allowing you to "refill your well." I ask my clients to practice self-care that nurtures them physically (e.g., exercise, massage); emotionally (e.g., connecting with a friend or support group); mentally (e.g., reading, surfing the Internet); and spiritually (e.g., praying, meditating, journaling). You probably won't be able to nurture all four areas each day, but treat yourself to at least weekly nurturing in all of them. And I'm a great believer in using little chunks of time to their best advantage. For instance, you could carry a book wherever you go. If there's an unexpected wait time somewhere, you could use it to enjoy whatever you're reading now rather than sitting there flipping through three-year-old magazines or fuming. Be creative! Look for ways to put **YOU** first on your calendar.

CHAPTER 9

> A master builder's tool chest is a thing of beauty—filled with just the right devices for many tasks, organized so that each is in its own place, clean and ready to use. How does your own tool chest compare? This chapter will teach you about another of the most important tools for life building: establishing and maintaining good habits.

The TOOL CHEST
Time & HABITS

I read a lot of self-help books, filled with great suggestions. I aim to write three pages each morning when I get up, as Julia Cameron in *The Artist's Way* recommends as an impetus to creativity. Or, as Oprah suggests, I try to write a gratitude list each day, or to do any of the other five or six things currently on my list of "I'd really feel better if I . . ."

You could add these good ideas to your calendar. But I have a tool I like better for tracking self-improvement activities. It's called "10 Daily Habits," which you'll see on page 118. I love this simple tool: a spreadsheet with the 28–31 days of the month across the top and one to ten habits that you want to track down the left side. It's a simple technique to help you track your progress on little (or not so little) habits you want to incorporate into your life.

In this chapter, we'll look at how establishing and maintaining good habits will keep you balanced and on track as you move forward toward your goals.

Habits

*W*hat we're going to look at now is habits that WILL help you be the best you can be—and that will help you remain balanced while you move forward toward your goals.

To best set yourself up for success, I suggest you tackle new behaviors one at a time. During the next twelve months, you can join The Habit-of-the-Month Club. Developing a great new habit each month is a way to renew yourself, and keep yourself energized, while letting it become part of your routine. Find out more on the next page!

The HABIT-OF-THE-MONTH Club

Ann's Habits

Month no./Habit of the Month

1. Workout at East Bank Club three times per week.

2. Do one daily anonymous act of kindness.

3. Read an article in trade magazines or business magazines each day.

4. Pray daily.

5. Take vitamins—daily.

6. Delegate to someone each day.

7. Be a communicative leader— speak up in meetings regularly.

8. Practice meditation.

9. Write three pages in my journal.

10. Clear clutter at work and home—15 minutes decluttering/day.

11. Follow food plan to stay slim over holidays.

12. Do something for family or close friends each day.

*I*t takes about a month for a new habit to become ingrained into your consciousness. I'd like for you to pick a habit to focus on in the next month that you will use to renew yourself. Then for each month following, pick a new habit to form. It may be physical (exercise, floss your teeth, eat five fruits/veggies per day); emotional (reach out to someone each day, write in journal); mental (read, take steps to learn something, go somewhere new on the Internet); or spiritual (meditate, pray daily, read inspirational literature).

Though I'll encourage you to form habits to keep you energized, I'd like your focus to be on developing that one Habit-of-the-Month. And by the way, the examples above are simply that—examples. I encourage people to continue with the habit once they've got it established. So don't let up on Month 1's habit in Month 2—in Month 1, your 10 Daily Habits may have one habit to track and by Month10 you'll have ten. Then you can decide which ones you either feel like letting go of, or that are so much part of your routine that you no longer need to track them (I'm like that with writing in my journal each morning, for instance—it's automatic with me now). Let's look at how Ann, a busy forty-something executive at a growing computer company mapped out her habits:

YOUR Turn

𝓕ill in the next month now. Stop there—let the others flow naturally as each month comes.

Once you have a habit in mind, you'll begin using the 10 Daily Habits form on page 119 to track your progress. As the months go by, you can add a new habit and still retain the old ones, if you'd like. Though there's space for up to ten habits, you could begin by just tracking one and work up. Experiment and see what works for you.

Month no. Habit of the Month

1 _____

2 _____

3 _____

4 _____

5 _____

6 _____

7 _____

8 _____

9 _____

10 _____

11 _____

12 _____

10 Daily Habits

*H*ere is Ann's record of her progress for the first half of the 12th month in her program. Notice how she has marked Saturdays and Sundays with an "S" as a reminder that she isn't asking herself to track all her habits on the weekends (although she may, if she chooses). She's decided incrementally to add a habit a month—so now, in Month 12, she is tracking her progress for twelve habits simultaneously. The chart shows her first ten habits for the first ten days of the month:

Habit	1	2	3	4	5	S	S	8	9	10	11	12	S	S	15	16	17	18	19	S	S	22	23	24	25	26	S	S	29	30	31
Workout at east Bank Club 3x/week	•		•		•			•		•																					
Reach out to someone daily	•	•		•				•	•	•																					
Read trade magazines and business magazines each day	•	•	•		•			•			•	•																			
Pray	•	•	•	•	•			•	•	•	•	•																			
Vitamins	•	•	•	•	•			•	•	•																					
Delegate	•			•	•			•	•	•																					
Be a communicative leader– speak up in meetings regularly	•	•		•		•		•	•																						
Meditate	•			•	•	•			•																						
Write in my journal first thing each morning			•		•	•	•			•	•																				
Clear clutter at work and home– 15 min de-cluttering/day	•	•	•					•	•	•																					

$\mathscr{T}$hink about the habits you've focused on developing. Perhaps, to begin with, you'll just want to track one habit (your "habit of the month."). Or maybe you're already working on several. Simply record your habit(s) in the space indicated, and then track your progress by putting an "x" under the date on days you succeed with that habit. (You may want to make copies of the form below so you can reuse it.)

Now it's YOUR turn!
10 Daily Habits for Month no. ....

Habit	1	2	3	4	5	S	S	8	9	10	11	12	S	S	15	16	17	18	19	S	S	22	23	24	25	26	S	S	29	30	31
1																															
2																															
3																															
4																															
5																															
6																															
7																															
8																															
9																															
10																															

The Dance:
STRUCTURE AND SPONTANEITY

Everyone gets the same number of hours in a week: 168. We each get the same 24 hours in a day. And each hour, for everyone, everywhere, contains 60 minutes. Why, then, does it seem as if some people have mastered time, while others experience it as their biggest impediment?

When I ask my coaching clients questions like "What is stopping you?" or "What's the biggest challenge you have in this situation?" they inevitably answer, "Time!"

People perceive that the lack of time to do what they want or need to do is the problem.

First of all, we don't lack time! It's there—like air. If it feels as if there isn't enough time, it's because you are already using the time that flows in your life, as you use the air you breathe. So first let's get clear that it is not the lack of time per se that is troubling you. It's the lack of time to do something specific.

Here's another thing to consider. Not all hours are created equally. What do I mean by that? Let me give you a few examples. How long do you suppose the following one-hour activities would feel?

- **The first hour at your wedding reception**
- **The last hour you spend with your dying mother**
- **The hour-long job interview for a job that you so ardently desire**

- **An hour-long coffee date with a blind date you wish you didn't have**
- **An hour-long coffee date with someone who sends sparks flying in the first five minutes**
- **The first hour of your new son's life**
- **An hour with that same infant son when he is colicky and screaming**

You get my point. All hours are not the same.

I once read a book on productivity and time management (that out of kindness shall remain anonymous) in which the author seriously urged his readers to schedule every moment of every day and focus on being productive. You may have the impression that I've been doing the same thing. If so, you couldn't be more wrong!

In fact, I agree with John Lennon: "Life is what happens to you when you're busy making other plans."

The point of *Be Your Own Life Coach* is to help you to focus on where you are, envision what you really want in life, and then map out structures and support to help you get from where you are to where you want to be. It is NOT to turn you into a time-slavish, robotic creature who is productive—yes—but massively unhappy with your lot.

The nature of life is not usually linear—at least not mine, my clients, or the lives of anyone I know! Life is yeasty, exciting, chaotic, and full.

There is a dance that occurs between structure and spontaneity, between order and chaos.

From media studies and friends of mine who are working moms, I have heard that the happiest women are those who divide their time between doing work they love and staying home with the kids they love. If indeed that is true, it would seem to be because they get the best of both worlds.

The same idea can be applied to this dance of structure and spontaneity. Yes, plan your work and work your plan, as my friend Bill says. AND leave room in your life, and your calendar, for life to erupt in all its glories.

My mentor in corporate life, Eric Dean, was a perfect model of this principle for me. He was incredibly productive, structured, and achievement oriented. He got a lot done. And he built a nearly fanatical following among the people he led by focusing first on people, then on tasks. For example, I remember one time when Eric was in the middle of some huge projects and the typical swell of corporate political maneuvering. On the way to a stressful meeting, he ran into my friend Pam in the elevator. At the time, Pam was in the throes of a painful divorce. She's a quiet woman. Private. And very dedicated to her work. Eric took one look at her and said, "You look like you're suffering, Pam. What's going on?" Since he had taken the time to forge personal relationships with those who worked for him, Pam took his question seriously and confided that her divorce was sad and challenging. Eric urged her to come to his office later in the day so they could talk.

Did Eric "have the time" to devote to connecting with Pam? If you mean in the sense of "Was his calendar devoid of meetings, was his to-do list devoid of tasks?" Well, no! He probably "didn't have time" until three months from Tuesday, for goodness sakes! But did he have the time to connect with someone personally, to share, if only for a short while, in the suffering and pain of another human being? He did.

His willingness to drop his schedule and be fully present when that was "the next right thing" to do was, I believe, one of the secret components of his phenomenal success. You see, those of us who worked for this man would have done, and regularly did do, just about anything for him. His secret business ingredient, I believe, was love.

Let that be true for you, too. When you're creating big plans and projects for yourself, remember who you are, who you want to be, what you value, and what you're really trying to do here.

Do you know the Harry Chapin song, "Cat's in the Cradle"? It tells of a busy father, always wanting to love and connect with his young son, but, as the song says, there were planes to catch and bills to pay—and his son learned to walk while his father was absent. By the end of the song, the tables have turned. The older dad, now retired, seeks connection with his son, who laments that he'd love to—if he could find the time. But his new job's a hassle and the kids are sick with flu . . .

Please! If you take one thing away from this part of the book, let this idea be it. It's hard to get to the life of your dreams without structure—visioning, planning, and then using your times and habits wisely to achieve your goals. But it's equally hard to have a life you love without spontaneity. It's important to know when to throw schedules and plans to the wind and focus on being, not doing.

It's a dance. Too much structure and you become a joyless robot. Not enough structure and you're awhirl in chaos, going nowhere fast. Dance!

CHAPTER 10

> Although I suppose it is possible for one person to build a big house, it doesn't sound like very much fun. Or the best use of your time either. World-class athletes, musicians, and business executives have long known one of the key secrets of success is having a crew of supportive people who will actively help them achieve their goals. You can, too.

My CREW

GETTING THE *Support* I NEED

You've already put a lot of work into Being Your Own Life Coach. Perhaps you're feeling excited. Maybe a little fearful. Possibly overwhelmed. My hunch would be that there may be some adrenaline going right now, ready to propel you forward, which is terrific. However, most things worth putting this much effort into will occur over time. And over time, it's easy to get discouraged, to get off track for a day, then two, then a week ... and then just give up.

If you have a support team, that is less likely to happen. In this chapter, you'll explore more about why support is crucial, what type of crew to recruit, and how to go about building YOUR winning team.

Why A SUPPORT TEAM is *Crucial*

I once heard former U.S. president Jimmy Carter interviewed on National Public Radio. The interviewer was describing him as a "self-made man" and making much of his rise from peanut farmer to president. But then President Carter corrected the interviewer, interjecting that, while he took full responsibility for his decisions and any mistakes he had made along the way, it would be unfair—and untrue—to claim his success as solely his own doing. He went on to recount some of the help he had received early in his farming, and then his political, career.

I was impressed by President Carter's honesty and integrity, but not surprised by what he said. To be successful in a big way, you need others. I remember my father telling me that one of the secrets of wealth was "OPM." When I asked, "What's OPM?" he smiled and said, "Other People's Money."

So, too, with success. Other People's Work. Other People's Ideas. Other People's Enthusiasm. Other People's Nudging. Other People's Resources. Other People's Networks. The list goes on and on, but the key is "Other People"!

Think about it. Picture a highly successful individual or person you admire. How many people are "on their team"?

On pages 128–129, we'll explore the types of people you'll want on your team. And then, on pages 130–131, you'll learn how to garner this support. We'll look at how these successful people do it—and how you can, too.

For now, let's explore a bit more **WHY** you'd want to have a support team.

You've set some big goals for yourself. You've mapped out a plan and have divided your big plan into day-sized chunks. That fluttering in your stomach when you think about all of this: Is it excitement? Or fear?

It's probably a bit of both, mixed in with some doubt—can I **REALLY** do this? There's a lot to do, and that's where your support team comes in.

This crew of recruited helpers can not only keep you motivated and remind you of **WHY** you wanted to do this in the first place, but they can also:

1. **Give you fresh ideas (and ideas can build synergistically)**
2. **Keep you accountable (this is why the buddy system works so well in exercising—when you commit to another person to do something you're more likely to follow through)**
3. **Help keep your focus on your big picture—your support system can help you hold your vision, especially when you are discouraged and caught up in life's little day-to-day dramas**
4. **Remind you of the next little steps to take**
5. **Cheer you on when you're on a roll—we ALL need enthusiastic supporters!**
6. **And console you when the going gets tough**

In short, your support team is the difference between success and failure in the "Do It!" part of this program. It's **THAT** important.

Now that you know **WHY** you'd want to recruit a crew, let's talk about some open positions on yours.

HELP Wanted

OPEN POSITIONS ON YOUR CREW

> A palatial estate outside London. A new high rise in Manhattan. A cottage by the sea in the Hebrides. A three-bedroom colonial in Minneapolis. Some elements of a building crew would be pretty consistent—you're likely to need a plumber on any of these projects. But some would require a more specialized crew.

*S*o, too, with your personal team. Some positions are pretty universal: Spouse/significant other/best friend/chief cheerleader—someone who loves you and encourages you is likely to enhance any goals you set.

Some team members, however, are specific to **YOUR** goals. Are you self-employed? A great accountant is one of your key support team members. And a good Webmaster might be, too.

Do your goals include physical prowess? Maybe having a personal trainer is wise for you.

Are you setting lofty financial goals? You, too, could use a great accountant, but a financial planner may be part of your team, and/or a terrific stockbroker.

Here are just a few ideas about the sort of help, and people you may want on **YOUR** personal support team:

1. **Personal support (spouse, best friend, family)**
2. **Legal issues (attorneys: real estate, tax, estate, divorce— as needed)**
3. **Finances (accountant, financial planner, banker, stockbroker)**
4. **Real estate (realtor, attorney, mortgage broker)**

5. **Your body (doctor, chiropractor, nutritionist, massage therapist, personal trainer)**
6. **Your space (professional organizer, housekeeper, handyman, personal assistant)**
7. **Your mental health (coach, spiritual advisor, therapist)**

Besides these role-based advisors, you're going to want people on your team who bring specific qualities, perhaps in addition to, or instead of, content expertise. So look for traits such as:

1. **Someone who DOES have content knowledge about your goal**
2. **Someone who is the most level-headed, clear thinker you know**
3. **Someone who is not afraid to tell you that you seem to be walking off the edge of a cliff**
4. **The eternal optimist**

Some Ideas
HOW BEST TO USE YOUR SUPPORT SYSTEM

*A*ll right. You know you need support. On the previous pages, you got some ideas on the types of people you want on your team. Now, write down the names of the people who came up, and why:

_____

_____

_____

_____

_____

_____

_____

_____

_____

_____

_____

_____

_____

_____

_____

Now that you have identified the people you want on your team, you can proceed in a few different ways:

Form a Personal Board of Directors

When I first heard of having a personal board of directors, I didn't know whether to dismiss the idea as another business/personal-growth fad, or embrace it with delight. While the phraseology is a bit too corporate-speak for me, the idea is terrific! Think about it: Corporations have boards to help them make key strategic decisions. Why shouldn't you? Here's how: After you've chosen the members, issue a formal invitation for them to join your personal board, explaining that you are forming a group of advisors to meet with periodically for strategic visioning and advice. Tell them why you're doing it, why you've invited them, and what you expect. Plan to meet with them regularly (quarterly is a good starting place). Keep the meetings focused (written agenda), on time, and upbeat. And feed them! If people are giving you their time, at least provide breakfast or lunch for them. Remember, the power of the group is that you have many minds helping you on one issue. Your accountant's perspective on whether or not to pursue piano lessons might surprise you. In fact, it was my accountant who first suggested that I write an earlier version of this book!

Form a Master-Mind Group

Alternatively, you could create a master-mind or success group with the people you've chosen. Napoleon Hill wrote about master-mind groups in his classic book from the 1930s, *Think and Grow Rich*. Essentially, this idea involves forming a small group of people with whom to have weekly meetings to encourage, motivate, and hold one another accountable.

The difference between this and a personal board is two-fold: the master-mind group tends to meet more often, and it provides accountability and support for **ALL** the members.

Have a Coaching Circle—or Choose One Specific Friend

A coaching circle can be set up where you coach Joe, Joe coaches Anne, Anne coaches Alice, and Alice coaches you. So you act as an informal peer-coach to someone, and someone else in the group is a peer-coach for you. You could easily do that using this book as your text. Alternatively, you could trade coaching with one friend—first you coach her and then she coaches you.

Start a Wisdom Circle

*O*r, you could start your own personal deepening group. Two marvelous books address having a circle of friends as a part of your personal growth path: *Calling the Circle* by Christina Baldwin and *Wisdom Circles* by Charles Garfield, Cindy Spring, and Sedonia Cahill. Essentially, the circles are, as Christina Baldwin points out, "a council of ordinary people who convene to create a sacred space and from that space accomplish a specific task, supporting each other in the process."

"Pay as You Go"—Hire these People

*O*ne other obvious way to get support is simply to form separate paid relationships. Hire your accountant to advise you financially, your therapist to give you emotional support, and your coach to help you clarify and pursue your goals (and hold you accountable while giving you support). I see coaching as a co-creative partnership in which the coach and the client work together to bring about the client's growth and greatest good through a process of deep listening, encouragement, and accountability. Choose a friend with whom you'd like to build that type of cocreative partnership.

However you do it, make sure you have someone else supporting you on your road to success!

Thomas Leonard, the founder of Coach U and arguably the father of the profession of coaching, once said, "Life is too short to have people around who don't believe in you." Get your team on board today—life is, indeed, short!

Taking Inventory

WHAT HAVE I LEARNED?

My former client Jim says, "Action leads to satisfaction." That's what Part Four was all about—the satisfaction of moving from ideas into manifestation. And not having to do it alone.

Chapter 8 focused on time-management skills, helping you move from large, mural-sized goals into small manageable drawings of the day to come.

Next, in Chapter 9, you focused on establishing (and maintaining) good habits. Did you take advantage of the offer to join The-Habit-of-the-Month Club?

Finally, in Chapter 10, I hope you were relieved to find that you don't have to DO it all by yourself—you can enlist the advice, aid, and encouragement of your support team.

Now stop and reflect on what you've learned from this part of the book.

Use these two pages to summarize what this part of the book has evoked. Are you energized about moving from ideas into action? Maybe you're thrilled to think of your own personal board of directors—or maybe the very thought makes you shrink into your shyness? Write about how this part of the book made you feel as you took the final preparations to move from dreaming it to doing it! Ask yourself questions like:

- Who is on my support team already?
- What form do I want my support to take? The Board of Directors? The Wisdom Circle? The Coaching Circle? How am I going to get the group started?
- What specialized positions do I want to fill on my team?
- How can I make this a win-win for the people I ask to support me so I'm more likely to get the support I need? What's in it for them?

PART 5

Wrap-up

& LIFE COACH CASE STUDIES

C ongratulations! You've progressed into Being Your Own Life Coach! In Part One, you began by looking at where you're at right now, and I suspect there may have been a few "Ahas!" as you saw first a visual representation of the balance in your life and then a clear view of the foundations you have built. Next, in Part Two, you looked at where you want to go in life. You created the big picture (even literally, I hope, with your Visionary Collage).

Part Three brought you back into the realm of the pragmatic and analytical. Here you took your broad vision and turned it into **I'M SMART** goals: goals that are Inner Motivated, Specific, Measurable, and Attainable and for which you have Resources and a Timetable. And you mapped how to achieve your goals—for the year, the next quarter, the month, the week, and day by day.

Part Four taught you techniques to move from planning to action, focusing on time management, good habits, and the magic ingredient to move you into success: having appropriate support.

Finally, in Part Five you will hear from people at various stages in life who are enjoying results as they put the tools in this book into action.

> **"May you be filled with loving kindness.**
> **May you be well.**
> **May you be peaceful and at ease.**
> **May you be happy."**
>
> *—Buddhist blessing*

My wish for you, dear reader, is that *Be Your Own Life Coach* has given you a plan to move toward a life of your dreams in the coming year. And that you return, again and again, to use these same tools because, as you know, during your life your goals and aspirations will change, but the tools for achieving them stay the same. My wish for you is not only achievement, but also serenity.

How do you learn things? For me, the best way is first to read about it. Then see how other people have done the same thing—either in person, or by reading about how they did it. Then I move into action. Read. Observe. Do.

You've done a lot of reading and a lot of work, but I suspect your ideal life, while underway, has not yet fully manifested. You may be wondering, "Did I do it right? Will this really work?"

This part of the book will introduce you to three people who have successfully used these same tools to move from dreaming a bigger dream to living a life they only imagined.

In Case Study 1, you'll meet Aaron. He's twenty-two, living at home after leaving a physics program at a prestigious university. Now he's interested in filmmaking. Find out how Aaron used the tools in this book to flesh out his dreams, come up with a plan, and prepare for action!

In Case Study 2, Pat recounts how she had to revision and remake her life after raising her three kids. Extremely bright and even more youthful and energetic—you wouldn't guess she's forty-nine—Pat is seeking, not only new visions, but a whole new support team as she moves into a totally different way of life. She is moving toward being a leader in the workplace as well as a wife and mother.

Finally, Case Study 3 presents Ann. In her mid-forties and a successful business executive, Ann had been searching for ways to really make a quantum leap at work **AND** at home. She recently married, travels constantly, and has taken the career risk of a lifetime. **AND** she wants to stay true to her core values. Find out how Ann managed her time, built a support network, and continued on to larger goals that fit into the context of her personal values.

Case Study 1 *Aaron*

Listen to how Aaron describes himself: "Twenty-two years old. Don't have a degree. Live at home with the folks. Work full-time as a banker. Don't have a girlfriend. In therapy. Balding. Not working out as much as I used to, but still look okay for now. Mildly depressed on occasion. Confused."

Earlier in his life, Aaron was interested in becoming a physicist, since he thought that field of study would help him to understand life.

When he enrolled in physics at a prominent university, here's what happened: "I found I was competing with the best and brightest minds of my generation. People who win Rhodes Scholarships. People who win Nobel Prizes." He froze. As he puts it, "I stopped performing at all. I just sat there. Not really doing anything. Which brings me to what I slowly came to realize."

Here's what he says about this awakening: "I realized I had the ambition to do art. More specifically, to do film. This was not some flash-in-the-pan thought straight out of left field. It has been in the back of my mind for quite some time." Now he's made some films. One he feels was a good learning opportunity, and the other, he's enthusiastic about. He's growing in his new field.

So this is where the tools you've seen in this book came in. I asked Aaron to use the tools presented to clarify his dream. Once he had done that work, we looked at what a plan for him to actually DO what he envisioned would look like. He got increasingly excited as his desires became clarified and he realized they were do-able.

Let's take a look at what he found:

Dream It!

When I asked Aaron to dream a bigger dream, here's what he said:

"So I'm a banker living at home without a degree. I'd like to be a filmmaker making work that is relevant and interesting. A degree would be nice, too.

"In my life's dream, I envision myself taking a week off work and flying out to the coast, where I present the screenplay I've just finished to some cynical development executive in Los Angeles. He tells me that my work is pretentious, yet promising. 'It'll only sell to the art-house types,' he says. 'They almost never break thirty mill domestic box-office gross—only once in a great while.' When I insist I want to make this movie I've written, he goes on, 'Why should I let you? What experience do you have? What kind of clout do you have in this town? Why should I pay you anything more than fifty grand (which is, by the way, the Writer's Guild minimum)?' But I fight right back: 'Because I understand the vision for this film better anyone else. Everyone's got to start someplace. You gonna let the guy who did Scooby-Doo do this thing? He's got more experience than me, but I'm better than he is, even though I haven't done anything yet. I'm better because I know I'm better. It's not arrogance. Just confidence.'

"Well, the guy likes my nerve. He doesn't see this often. Everyone tends to cower. I didn't. He gives me five million and a crew! I make the movie. Gets good reviews from reviewers that like pretentious art-house fare. Does well enough at the box office to let me do another one. That's the dream."

Plan It!

So, I felt pretty excited about Aaron's dreams too! We both really felt we could SEE him as a successful filmmaker—and that's important. We both believed in his dreams and really could get enthused.

But you know, while that's an important step toward manifesting our desires, it is only the beginning.

I said, "So, Aaron—how do you suppose you can bring this beautiful dream into reality? Where do you begin? What's the foundation for you to stand on here?"

I was delighted when he replied, "I actually already have written a full-length screenplay."

"Wow!" I said. "So that's great! So how does it go from being a script to being a film? Tell me what you've thought about there. Aaron's enthusiasm grew as he said "I'm thinking that I'll take a week off work in the summer to shoot and utilize a crew from the student filmmaking society at The University of Chicago. I'll draw my actors from local theater groups and schools. It won't be a Hollywood production, but I've already made two that weren't, either. I'll show it to whomever is willing to watch, submit it to festivals, and the like. Do my best to get noticed. After I make this film, I'm going to finish my degree.

"I may not ever really want to do it, but I think it's important, so I will. This is my plan."

In Aaron's case, clearly articulating his dream revealed that he really had a lot of his plans mapped out. But that's not always the case. However, sometimes, once the dream is clear it CAN be this easy to map out the next steps.

But what happens after that? You've got a dream. You know what to do next. Then you hit a snag. What happens then?

Do It!

"I'm in the process of implementing my strategy every day of my life. I've been writing and rewriting this script so many times that I've got it memorized. Do it? I AM doing it! Everything I can to make my dreams a living reality."

Aaron's lucky. He's young. He lives at home. His mom and dad (and, on good days, his kid brother) are incredibly supportive. He knows and hangs out with some really smart people who don't see any reason why all of them can't become incredibly famous, successful, and happy. So, in a sense he HAS the support system to back up his dreaming and planning. Aaron WILL do it!

Case Study 2 *Pat*

Pat faced a dilemma that many of my friends do. Many women I know are now either returning to the work force after having stayed home to raise a family, or they are seeking full-time work or work with more responsibility now that their child-rearing responsibilities have changed.

Pat and I have been friends for thirty-three years. She has three incredible kids of her own and two stepchildren. Though they aren't all "launched" by any means, her role as a mom is shifting and changing. One of the smartest people I know, Pat's intellectual acumen, enthusiasm, and passion for life can make her restless when her energies aren't fully engaged. A superb homemaker and world-class gardener, Pat would actually be happy to throw her energies into her home life.

But both economic realities and sensibilities about making a contribution around issues of justice for children and women have led Pat to reenter the larger world of work in a different way.

Pat has been working outside the home since her divorce from her former husband. She's had to balance child care and maintaining a large home and very large yard and garden with the jobs she has had. After the divorce, she got her master's degree in social work and took on the job of heading a social services agency. For a while she worked for a mortgage company, primarily to raise money to support herself and her three kids.

Dream It!

Pat has tremendous visioning skills. She can look at situations and clearly see what needs to be done and how to do it. But, like most of us, the path gets murkier when the strategy needed is a plan that works for her own life.

Plan It!

I've explained that you can gain support, wisdom, and insight by bringing your friends onboard your support team. Pat and I didn't coach per se but our long-term friendship provided a safe space for Pat to question what was next in her life. She was able to articulate what was missing. She understood that setting goals or priorities in her VERY busy schedule made more sense if those goals were driven by her values. Though the mortgage business was lucrative, it didn't speak to Pat's soul, or satisfy her passion for justice and the well-being of women and children.

Pat and I talked a lot about the alternatives open to her. I asked her: "What do you think matters the most when you're thinking about what options to pursue?" Pat and I both laughed when she told me that it wasn't just her values that she needed to honor, it was her personal style too. "What do YOU mean by that?" I asked. She said, "It's not just my values that I need to honor—it's also my personality quirks. I'm rather blunt and independent, you know!" We both laughed, because Pat DOES need to be able to "speak her piece" and go her own way. She's a strong-minded woman. I reminded her, too, "Pat you are also a deep thinker. Not only are you really smart, but you like to probe deeply into things. Not everyone does, you know." Because Pat understood her priorities—she had found out what she valued and what was important—when a friend called to ask if she'd act as a paid consultant to a social service agency, she sprang at the chance. She'd done the footwork to know what she was looking for. She had support and encouragement—from her current husband, her family, me, and her other friends.

Do It!

Pat still juggles many people and priorities. Her life, like that of many women her age, is very rich, and some days it feels almost TOO full. She knows her foundations. She's clear on her values. She knows what she wants out of life. And she knows how to bring joy and balance back into it.

Part of the benefit of middle age is that you DO have foundations. Most of us ARE clearer on our values and priorities. The tools in this book help you to make explicit what you probably already know. Once you know the ground you're standing on, getting clear on where you need to go next is easier.

If you need any further encouragement, just ask Pat! She says of this whole process: "With the help of coaching, I've realized that I had to adjust my priorities. In order to keep making money to pay my bills, I've learned to say 'no' sometimes when people ask for my insight and help."

Case Study 3 *Ann*

I wish you could meet Ann! She's a phenomenal woman, an impressive executive, and one of the most generous, big-hearted people I've met. Ann is also my longest-standing coaching client and has become my friend. Over the five-plus years that we've been regularly coaching, I've watched her grow exponentially.

Ann has worked through the tools in this book several times as she sets bigger and bigger goals for herself. When she first hired me, she seemed to be in a slump. Her life was not at all the way she wanted it to be. Ann has strong core values and a deep knowledge of herself and others. She knew that she could do—and BE—more than she was.

Dream It!

So our first step was "dreaming a bigger dream." At that point Ann was living in a rented apartment in our little town, was a partner in a small architectural design firm, and was dating her long-time beau. She was very frustrated at work, felt as if her personal and professional growth had stalled, and knew she could be making a bigger contribution in the world—and making a lot more money relative to the hours she was working, too.

I asked her to really stretch and imagine what she wanted in life.

Plan It!

So we began to look for a broader vision for Ann. Simultaneously, to help her get some needed concentration and focus for her goals, we took on the task of "clearing the brush." "What's in the way, Ann?" I asked? She could see some physical impediments, but she couldn't seem to get clear

on what was REALLY stopping her. We both knew she was smart, hard-working and deserved more from life.

For Ann, this mostly meant realizing there were people in her life who seriously breached her boundaries and were MAJOR energy drains. She identified these people and began to eliminate them from her life. She set stronger personal boundaries.

We talked about her dreams and not only what she'd need to eliminate to achieve them, but also what (and who) she'd need to add.

Do It!

With my encouragement, belief in her, and support, Ann realized that she needed to play on a bigger stage. She went from being an underutilized, undercompensated partner in a small firm to being a director at a highly respected global consulting company.

In these past few years, Ann has changed jobs again—now she is a vice president at an innovative business services company. *More important than the impressive title and big salary is that Ann is doing work at which she excels and that honors some of her core values such as integrity, relationship building, and continual personal growth.*

Additionally, during this time, Ann has bought the beautiful, big house of her dreams out in the country near our little town, married her long-time beau, Joe, and gotten her MBA at one of America's most impressive graduate schools.

Coaching tips

Here are some of the coaching tools Ann has used repeatedly to get herself here:

1. Assessing her foundations honestly. Particularly at the beginning of our work together, Ann took an honest look at where she was starting from.

2. Envisioning her goals, including doing Visionary Collages (she is a talented artist!). And Ann continues to "dream a bigger dream." She builds on her vision as she creates her life.

3. Removing those people, places, things, or habits that got in her way. In Ann's case, the primary focus was on people, but also on some less-than-helpful mental habits she had—habits like self-criticism, self-doubt, and lack of confidence.

As Ann's personal and professional life continued to expand, she and I have worked together consistently to help her map out specific, measurable goals for each year, for quarterly planning, etc. Last year we did a "Year of Leadership Growth" coaching curriculum in which each month we focused on a specific area of Ann's development as a business leader.

Support

In Ann's case having a long-term coaching relationship has provided her with ongoing support, but she has also worked hard at establishing a vital support system with strong family ties that she strives to maintain. And she has developed strong personal and professional friendships.

She was encouraged by her business mentor to apply for the MBA graduate program. This was a smart move for Ann and a clear step toward helping her achieve senior executive status. However, Ann didn't stop there. She networked l ike crazy, befriended her fellow students, and took a leadership role in class and in alumni activities. In so doing, she greatly expanded, not just her business network, but her own support system.

Ann also defined what SHE needed in support. She took the lead on redefining our coaching relationship so that it more aptly served her needs. We meet on Sunday mornings, when she is in town, for an extended session focusing on high-level goals, self-care, and support. We target our focus and work on specific areas that will most help Ann grow and be her best self.

Is it working? Ask Ann! She says: "From the beginning of my coaching experience, the reading, thinking, writing exercises, and discussions continued to evolve and expand as I worked on each new life challenge. We started with a life vision and assessment of transferable skills for a new career to a study of sophisticated leadership principles needed for an executive in a fast growing, global company. I could never have achieved as much as I have without the sage guidance, and encouragement to keep growing, that I have received."

Bibliography

Life Mission

Levoy, Gregg. Callings: *Finding and Following an Authentic Life.* New York: Three Rivers Press, 1998.

Personal Growth

Baldwin, Christina. *Calling the Circle: The First and Future Culture.* New York: Bantam Books, 1994.

Baldwin, Christina. *Life's Companion: Journal Writing as a Spiritual Quest.* New York: Bantam Books, 1991.

Cameron, Julia. *The Artist's Way, a Spiritual Path to Higher Creativity.* New York: Jeremy P. Tarcher/ Putnam, 1992.

Covey, Stephen. *The Seven Habits of Highly Effective People.* New York: Simon and Schuster, 1989.

Garfield, Charles, Cindy Spring, and Sedonia Cahill. Wisdom Circles: *A Guide to Self-Discovery and Community Building in Small Groups.* New York: Hyperion, 1998.

Hardin, Dr. Paula. *What Are You Doing with the Rest of Your Life: Choices in Midlife.* Novato, Calif: New World Library, 1992.

Kasl, Charlotte. *If the Buddha Dated: A Handbook for Finding Love on a Spiritual Path.* New York: Penguin Compass, 1999.

Mossbridge, Julia. *Unfolding: The Perpetual Science of Your Soul's Work.* Novato, Calif: New World Library, 2002.

Noble, Vicki. *Shakti Woman: Feeling Our Fire, Healing Our World.* San Francisco: Harper San Francisco, 1991.

Sher, Barbara. Wishcraft: *How to Get What You Really Want.* New York: Ballantine, 1979.

Spirituality

Kornfield, Jack. *After the Ecstasy, the Laundry: How The Heart Grows Wise on the Spiritual Path.* New York: Bantam Books, 2000.

Lamott, Anne. *Traveling Mercies: Some Thoughts on Faith.* New York: Anchor Books, 2000.

Muller, Wayne. *How Then Shall We Live: Four Simple Questions that Reveal the Beauty and Meaning of Our Lives.* New York: Bantam Books, 1996.

Kabat-Zinn, Jon. *Wherever You Go, There You Are.* New York: St. Martin's Press, 1994.

Williamson, Marianne. *A Return to Love: Reflections on the Principles of A Course in Miracles.* New York: HarperPerennial, 1992.

Work/Career/Money

Boldt, Laurence G. *Zen and the Art of Making a Living: A Practical Guide to Creative Career Design.* New York: Penguin Compass, 1999.

Mundis, Jerrold. *Making Peace with Money.* Kansas City: Andrew McNeel Publishing, 1999.

Nemeth, Maria. *The Energy of Money: A Spiritual Guide to Financial and Personal Fulfillment.* New York: Ballantine Wellspring, 1997.

Winter, Barbara J. *Making a Living Without a Job: Winning Ways For Creating Work That You Love.* New York: Bantam Books, 1993.